SAVED BY LIGHT

SAVED BY THE
LIGHT

DANNION BRINKLEY
WITH PAUL PERRY
WITH AN INTRODUCTION BY DR RAYMOND MOODY

BCA

LONDON   NEW YORK   SYDNEY   TORONTO

This edition published 1994
by BCA by arrangement with
Judy Piatkus (Publishers) Ltd

CN 4009

Printed in Great Britain

*This book is dedicated to the doctors,
nurses, and volunteers who perform the valuable
work of hospice.*

*Also to my family, the Brinkleys,
and especially to Dr. Raymond Moody.*

Contents

Introduction

I first read of Dannion Brinkley in an article in an Augusta, Georgia, newspaper. The story reported that a young man in a nearby South Carolina community had been struck in the head by lightning while talking on the telephone and had been miraculously resuscitated from a cardiac arrest. He was still alive but was hanging by a thread. He was in very critical condition, and it sounded as though he might not survive.

The year was 1975, and my book *Life After Life* was about to be published. I remember wondering at the time if he had had a near-death experience. I filed the newspaper article away, thinking that sometime in the future I would check on his status and perhaps even look him up if he were still alive.

As it happened, it was he who looked me up.

I was giving a lecture at a community college in South Carolina on near-death experiences and my studies of people who had had these deeply spiritual experiences while on the threshold of death. During the discussion period at the end of the talk, Dannion raised his hand and told of his experience. He held the audience spellbound with his dramatic story. He told the people in the room that he had left his body after being "killed" by lightning and journeyed to a spiritual realm where love permeates everything and knowledge is as accessible as air. As he told his story, I suddenly realized that this was the young man I had read about in the newspaper.

Afterward, I made an appointment to interview him and went to his home to listen to his story. To this day, Dannion Brinkley's near-death experience stands as one of the most remarkable I have heard. He saw his own dead body twice, when he left it and when he returned, and in between he went to a spiritual realm populated by kind and powerful beings who allowed him to see his life in full review and assess his own successes and failures. Then he went to a beautiful city of crystal and light and sat in the presence of thirteen Beings of Light who filled him with knowledge.

Most amazing was the type of knowledge to which they exposed him. In the presence of these spiritual beings, Dannion said, he was allowed a glimpse of the future.

He told me what he saw, all of which I considered to be nonsense, the ravings of a man fried by lightning. For instance, he told me that the breakdown of the Soviet Union would occur in 1989 and would be marked by food riots. He even told of a great war in the deserts of the Middle East that would be fought when a small country was invaded by a large one. According to the Beings of Light, there would be a clashing of two armies, one of which would be destroyed. This war would take place in 1990, Dannion insisted. The war he was talking about was, of course, the Gulf War.

As I have already said, I considered his predictions to be pure nonsense. Over the years I have just nodded and written down what he has said. For a long time I thought that his brain was somewhat scrambled by the incident, and I was willing to give him a considerable amount of latitude. After all, I reasoned, who wouldn't be a little strange after being struck by lightning?

Later it was I who acted like a person struck by lightning when I realized that the events he had told me about were coming true! How could this be? I wondered. How could a near-death experience lead to the capacity to see into the future? I didn't know the answer.

I have been a close friend of Dannion since we first talked in 1976. In those intervening years another revelation has made me feel as if I have been struck by lightning. Dannion Brinkley appears to be able to read minds!

He has done this many times with me—simply looked me right in the eyes and told me what was going on in the most personal aspects of my life. More important, I have seen him apparently read the minds of total strangers, telling them what they received in the mail that very day, who telephoned them, or how they felt about their spouses, children, even themselves.

He doesn't do this in the form of vague proclamations. Rather, he is incredibly specific. He once came into a college classroom where I was teaching and knew details of the personal lives of every student in the room! He was so accurate and specific in his readings that all the class members were gasping and some were openly weeping at his revelations. I must point out here that he had never spoken to a single one of the students before entering the room. They were all strangers.

I have seen him "read the minds" of perfect strangers so many times that it has become almost commonplace in my life. In fact, I have come to cherish that moment of recognition when a person's skepticism is replaced by awe, then wonder, at the realization that his most private thoughts are being read like an open book.

How is it possible that a person who has a near-death experience is suddenly able to read minds and predict the future?

In his book *Transformed by the Light,* Dr. Melvin Morse describes a study he conducted that shows that people who have had near-death experiences (NDEs) have three times the number of verifiable psychic experiences as do those who have never had NDEs. Their psychic abilities are not as profound as those displayed by Dannion, but they are measurable nonetheless. This study verifies others like it and proves that there is something about these deeply spiritual experiences that stimulates extrasensory perceptions in the people who have them.

In the end, I admit to being stymied by Dannion Brinkley. At the same time, I am somewhat comforted by his story. It is, after all, a mystery, but mysteries like this one propel us forward in search of answers.

Raymond Moody, M.D.

Saved
by the
Light

1

The First Time I Died

About five minutes before I died, I could hear the roll of thunder as another storm marched into Aiken, South Carolina. Out the window I could see lightning streak across the sky, making that sizzling sound before hitting the ground with a pop—"artillery from God," someone in my family had called it. Over the years I had heard dozens of stories about people and animals being struck and killed by lightning. The lightning stories my great-uncle would tell at night when the summer storms rumbled in and the room would strobe with bright flashes were as scary to me as ghost stories. That fear of lightning had never left me. Even on this

3

night, September 17, 1975, at the age of twenty-five, I wanted to get off the telephone quickly to avoid a "phone call from God." (I think it was also my great-uncle who used to say, "Remember, if you get a phone call from God, you usually become the burning bush," but I am sure he meant it as a joke.)

"Hey Tommy, I've got to get going, a storm's coming."

"So what?" he said.

I had been home from a trip to South America for only a few days and had planted myself on the telephone. I worked for the government and was also involved in several business concerns of my own. I owned and rented a number of houses, bought and repaired old cars, helped in my family's grocery business, and was in the process of starting a company. As the rain fell outside, I had to finish this last phone call to a business partner.

"Tommy, I gotta go. Mother always told me never to talk on the phone during a thunderstorm."

And that was it. The next sound I heard was like a freight train coming into my ear at the speed of light. Jolts of electricity coursed through my body, and every cell of my being felt as if it were bathed in battery acid. The nails of my shoes were welded to the nails in the floor so that when I was thrown into the air, my feet were pulled out of them. I saw the ceiling in front of my face, and for a moment I couldn't imagine what power it was that could cause such searing pain and hold me in its grip, dangling over my own bed. What must have been a split second seemed like an hour.

Somewhere down the hall my wife Sandy had shouted, "That was a close one," when she heard the thunder. But I didn't hear her say that, I only found out about it much later. I also didn't see the horrified look on her face as she peered down the hall and saw me hanging in midair. For a moment all I saw was the plaster of the ceiling.

Then I went into another world.

From immense pain I found myself engulfed by peace and tranquility. It was a feeling I had never known before and have not had since. It was like bathing in a glorious calmness. This place that I went to was an atmosphere of deep blue and gray where I was actually able to relax for a moment and wonder just what it was that had hit me so hard. Had a plane crashed into the house? Was our country under nuclear attack? I had no idea what had happened, but even in this moment of peacefulness I wanted to know where I was.

I began to look around, to roll over in midair. Below me was my own body, thrown across the bed. My shoes were smoking and the telephone was melted in my hand. I could see Sandy run into the room. She stood over the bed and looked at me with a dazed expression, the kind you might find on the parent of a child found floating facedown in a swimming pool. She quivered for a moment and then went to work. She had recently taken a course in cardiopulmonary resuscitation and knew exactly what to do. First she cleared my throat and moved my tongue to the side, then she tilted my head back and began to breathe into my mouth. One—two—three breaths and then she straddled my stomach and began pushing on my chest. She was pushing so hard that she grunted with each downward stroke.

I must be dead, I thought. I could feel nothing because I was not in my body. I was a spectator of my final moments on earth, as dispassionate about watching my own death as I might be if I were watching actors reenact it on television. I felt sorry for Sandy and could feel her fear and pain, but I was not concerned about that person lying on the bed. I do recall one thought that shows how far from pain I was. As I gazed at the man on the bed I remember thinking, I thought I was better looking than that.

The CPR must have worked because I was suddenly back in my body. Above me I could feel Sandy pounding on my chest. Normally, such bone-cracking pressure would be painful, but I did not feel it. The electricity had coursed through my body, and there wasn't a single spot on me that didn't feel as if it had been burned from the inside out. I began to moan, but only because I was too weak to scream.

Tommy showed up in less than ten minutes. He knew something was wrong because he had heard the explosion over the telephone. He had been a Navy corpsman so Sandy let him take over. He wrapped me in a blanket and told her to call the emergency medical unit. "We'll do what we can," he said, placing his hand on my chest.

By now I had left my body again, and I watched as Tommy held me and cursed the slowness of the ambulance, which we could hear approaching in the distance. I hovered above the three of them—Sandy, Tommy, and myself—as the medical technicians loaded me onto the stretcher and wheeled me to the ambulance.

From where I hovered, about fifteen feet above everyone, I could see the pouring rain hitting my face and drenching the backs of the ambulance crew. Sandy was crying and I felt sorry for her. Tommy was speaking quietly to the crew. They slid me into the ambulance, closed the doors, and took off.

The perspective I had was that of a television camera. Without passion or pain, I watched as the person on the stretcher began to twitch and jump. Sandy was pressed against the side of the ambulance, withdrawing in terror from the sight of the man she loved convulsing on the stretcher before her. The emergency medical technician injected something in the body, hoping for some positive result, but after several seconds of painful convulsions, the man on the stretcher stopped moving. The technician put a stethoscope to his chest and let out a sigh.

"He's gone," he said to Sandy. "He's gone."

All of a sudden it hit me: That man on the stretcher was me! I watched as the technician pulled a sheet over my face and sat back. The ambulance didn't slow down, and the technician in the front seat was still on the radio to the hospital, trying to find out if there was anything the doctors wanted them to do. But the man on the stretcher was clearly dead.

I am dead! I thought. I was not in my body and can honestly say that I didn't want to be. If I had any thought at all, it was simply that who I was had nothing to do with that body they had just covered with a sheet.

Sandy was sobbing and patting my leg. Tommy was stunned and feeling overwhelmed at the suddenness of this event. The emergency medical technician was looking only at the body and feeling like a failure.

Don't feel bad, buddy, I thought. It ain't your fault.

I looked toward the front of the ambulance to a spot over my dead body. A tunnel was forming, opening like the eye of a hurricane and coming toward me.

That looks like an interesting place to be, I thought. And away I went.

2

The Tunnel
to Eternity

I actually didn't move at all; the tunnel came to me.
There was the sound of chimes as the tunnel spiraled
toward and then around me. Soon there was nothing to be
seen—no crying Sandy, no ambulance attendants trying to
jump-start my dead body, no desperate chatter with the hospital over the radio—only a tunnel that engulfed me completely
and the intensely beautiful sound of seven chimes ringing in
rhythmic succession.

I looked ahead into the darkness. There was a light up there,
and I began to move toward it as quickly as possible. I was
moving without legs at a high rate of speed. Ahead the light

became brighter and brighter until it overtook the darkness and left me standing in a paradise of brilliant light. This was the brightest light I had ever seen, but in spite of that, it didn't hurt my eyes in the least. Unlike the pain one might feel when walking into sunlight from a dark room, this light was soothing to my eyes.

I looked to my right and could see a silver form appearing like a silhouette through mist. As it approached I began to feel a deep sense of love that encompassed all of the meanings of the word. It was as though I were seeing a lover, mother, and best friend, multiplied a thousandfold. As the Being of Light came closer, these feelings of love intensified until they became almost too pleasurable to withstand. I had the sense of becoming less dense, as though I had lost twenty or thirty pounds. The burden of my body had been left behind, and now I was an unencumbered spirit.

I looked at my hand. It was translucent and shimmering and moved with fluidity, like the water in the ocean. I looked down at my chest. It, too, had the translucence and flow of fine silk in a light breeze.

The Being of Light stood directly in front of me. As I gazed into its essence I could see prisms of color, as though it were composed of thousands of tiny diamonds, each emitting the colors of the rainbow.

I began to look around. Below us were other Beings who looked like me. They appeared to be lost and shimmered at a rate that was far slower than the rate at which I shimmered. As I watched them I noticed that I slowed down as well. There was a discomfort in this reduced vibration that made me look away.

I looked above me. There were more Beings, these brighter and more radiant than I. I felt discomfort when looking at them as well because I began to vibrate faster. It was as though I had drunk too much coffee and was now speeding up and moving too fast. I looked away from them and straight ahead at the Being of Light, who now stood before me. I felt comfortable in his presence, a familiarity that made me believe he had felt every feeling I had ever had, from the time I took my first breath to the instant I was sizzled by lightning. Looking at this Being I had the feeling that no one could love me better, no one could have more empathy, sympathy, encouragement, and nonjudgmental compassion for me than this Being.

Although I refer to the Being of Light as a "he," I never saw this Being as either male or female. I have gone over this initial meeting many times in my head and can honestly say that none of the Beings I met had gender, just great power.

The Being of Light engulfed me, and as it did I began to experience my whole life, feeling and seeing everything that had ever happened to me. It was as though a dam had burst and every memory stored in my brain flowed out.

This life review was not pleasant. From the moment it began until it ended, I was faced with the sickening reality that I had been an unpleasant person, someone who was self-centered and mean.

The first thing I saw was my angry childhood. I saw myself torturing other children, stealing their bicycles or making them miserable at school. One of the most vivid scenes was of the time I picked on a child at grade school because he had a goiter that protruded from his neck. The other kids in the class picked on him too, but I was the worst. At the time I thought I was funny. But now, as I relived this incident, I found myself in his body, living with the pain that I was causing.

This perspective continued through every negative incident in my childhood, a substantial number to be sure. From fifth to twelfth grade, I estimate that I had at least six thousand fistfights. Now, as I reviewed my life in the bosom of the Being, I relived each one of those altercations, but with one major difference: I was the receiver.

I wasn't the receiver in the sense that I felt the punches I had thrown. Rather, I felt the anguish and the humiliation my opponent felt. Many of the people I fought had it coming, but others were innocent victims of my anger. Now I was forced to feel their pain.

I also felt the grief I had caused my parents. I had been uncontrollable and proud of it. Although they had grounded me and yelled at me, I had let them know by my actions that none of their discipline really mattered. Many times they had pleaded with me and many times they had met frustration. I had often bragged to my friends about how I had hurt my parents. Now, in my life review, I felt their psychological pain at having such a bad child.

My grade school in South Carolina had a demerit system. Students who received 15 demerits had their parents called in for a conference, while those who had 30 demerits on their record were suspended. In seventh grade, I had received 154 demerits by the third day of school. I was that kind of student. Now they call students like that "hyperactive" and do something about it. Back then we were just called "bad kids" and were thought to be lost causes.

When I was in the fourth grade, a redheaded boy named

Curt would wait for me every day before school and threaten to beat me up if I didn't give him my lunch money. I was afraid, and gave him the money.

Finally, I got tired of going all day without eating and told my father what was happening. He showed me how to make a blackjack out of a pair of my mother's nylon stockings by pouring sand into them and tying the ends. "When he bothers you again, hit him with the blackjack," he told me.

My father didn't mean any harm—he was just showing me how to protect myself from the older kids. The problem was that after I bludgeoned Curt and took his money, I developed a taste for fighting. From that point on, all I wanted to do was inflict pain and be tough.

When I was in the fifth grade I polled all my friends to find out who they thought was the toughest kid in the neighborhood. They all agreed that it was a stocky kid named Butch. I walked up to his house and knocked on the door. "Is Butch here?" I asked his mother. When he came out the door I beat him until he fell off the porch, and then I ran away.

I didn't care who I fought, or how big or old they were. All I wanted to do was draw blood.

Once, in sixth grade, a teacher asked me to stop disrupting class. When I refused, she grabbed my arm and began marching me toward the principal's office. As we walked out of the classroom, I pulled loose and hit her with an uppercut that knocked her to the ground. As she held her bleeding nose, I walked myself to the principal's office. As I explained to my parents, I didn't mind going to the office, I just didn't want to be pulled there by a teacher.

We lived next door to the junior high school I attended, and

I could sit on the porch and watch the kids in the playground on the days that I was suspended from school. One day I was sitting there when a group of girls came to the fence and started making fun of me. I wasn't going to take that. I went into the house, got my brother's shotgun, and loaded it with rock salt. Then I came back out and shot the girls in the back as they fled, screaming.

By the time I was seventeen, I was known as one of the best fighters in my high school. I fought almost daily to maintain my reputation. When I couldn't find kids from my own school to beat up, I relied on the bad kids from other schools for competition.

At least once a week we had staged fights in a parking lot near school. Students would come from as far as thirty miles away to participate in these fights. On the days that I fought, many of the kids wouldn't get out of their cars, because after I beat up my opponent, I would take on a few spectators just for fun.

These were the days of segregated high schools, and we would have great wars between blacks and whites.

The black champion was a giant named Lundy. No one wanted to fight him after he beat the white champion in a savage two-minute battle. Even I tried to avoid him, knowing there was no way that I could win.

One day we ran into each other at a hamburger stand. I tried to leave quickly but he stepped in my way.

"Meet me tomorrow morning at the parking lot," he said.

"I'll be there," I promised. Then, as he turned to walk away, I hit him with such force on the right side of the face that he couldn't open his eyes for at least ten minutes. As he lay struggling on the ground, I walked around him and kicked him in the chest a couple of times as hard as I could.

"I won't be able to make it tomorrow," I said. "So I thought I would take care of it today."

I knew I couldn't beat him in a fair fight, so I jumped him when his back was turned.

That was the world I lived in through high school.

Twenty years later, at my high school reunion, a classmate cornered my date to tell her what kind of student I had been.

"Let me tell you what he was famous for," he said. "He would beat your ass, steal your girlfriend, or do both."

In retrospect, I couldn't have agreed with him more. By the time I was finished with high school, that is exactly who I was. And by the time I had reached that point in my review, I was ashamed of myself. Now I knew the pain I had caused everyone in my life. As my body lay dead on that stretcher, I was reliving every moment of my life, including my emotions, attitudes, and motivations.

The depth of emotion I experienced during this life review was astonishing. Not only could I feel the way both I and the other person had felt when an incident took place, I could also feel the feelings of the next person they reacted to. I was in a chain reaction of emotion, one that showed how deeply we affect one another. Luckily, not all of it was bad.

One time, for instance, my great-uncle and I were driving down the road when we saw a man beating a goat that had somehow gotten its head stuck in a fence. The man had a branch, and he was hitting the goat across the back as hard as he could while the goat bleated in fear and agony. I stopped the car and jumped across a ditch. Before the man could turn around, I was pounding him as hard as I could in the back of the head. I only stopped when my great-uncle pulled me off, I freed the goat and we left in a cloud of burnt rubber.

Now, as I relived that incident, I felt satisfaction at the humiliation that farmer had felt and joy in the relief the goat had felt. I knew that in the animal's own way, he had said "thank you."

But I wasn't always kind to animals. I saw myself whipping a dog with a belt. I had caught this dog chewing on our living room carpet and lost my temper. I had pulled my belt off and let him have it without trying a lesser form of discipline. Reliving this incident, I felt the dog's love for me and could tell that he didn't mean to do what he was doing. I felt his sorrow and pain.

Later, as I thought about these experiences, I realized that people who beat animals or are cruel to them are going to know how those animals felt when they have a life review.

I also discovered that it is not so much what you do that counts, but why you do it. For example, having a fistfight with someone for no real reason hurt me far more in the life review than having one with someone who had picked a fight with me. To relive hurting someone just for fun is the greatest pain of all. To relive hurting someone for a cause you believe in is not as painful.

This became obvious to me when my review took me back through my years in military and intelligence work.

In the span of what must have been a few seconds, I went through basic training, where I learned to channel my anger into my new role as a combat soldier. On through special training I went, watching and feeling my character being molded for the purpose of killing. This was the era of the Vietnam War, and I found myself back in the muggy jungles of Southeast Asia doing what I liked to do most—fight.

I spent very little time in Vietnam. I was attached to an intelligence unit that operated mainly in Laos and Cambodia. I did a bit of "observation work," which amounted to little more than watching enemy troop movements through binoculars. My main job was to "plan and execute the removal of enemy politicians and military personnel." In short, I was an assassin.

I didn't operate alone. Two other Marines worked with me as we scoured the jungles looking for specific targets. Their jobs was to spot the target with a high-powered telescope and verify that the desired person had been eliminated. My job was to pull the trigger.

Once, for example, we were sent to "terminate" a North Vietnamese colonel who was with his troops in the jungles of Cambodia. Aerial photographs showed us where this colonel was holed up. It was our job to tramp through the jungle and find him. Although this kind of attack was especially time consuming, it was considered crucial, for it broke the morale of the enemy troops to have their leader killed in their midst.

We found the colonel right where the maps said we would. We sat quietly about seven hundred yards from their camp, waiting for the perfect moment to "drop" him.

That moment came early the next morning, when the troops lined up for their daily review. I got into position, bringing the crosshairs of my high-powered sniper rifle on the head of the colonel, who was standing before the unsuspecting soldiers.

"Is that him?" I asked the spotter, whose job it was to identify the targets with the photographs intelligence had given us.

"That's him," he said. "The man standing right before the troops is him."

I squeezed off the round and felt the rifle kick. A moment later I saw his head explode and his body crumple before the shocked troops.

That is what I saw when the incident happened.

During my life review, I experienced this incident from the perspective of the North Vietnamese colonel. I didn't feel the pain that he must have felt. Instead, I felt his confusion at having his head blown off and sadness as he left his body and realized that he would never go home again. Then I felt the rest of the chain reaction—the sad feelings of his family when they realized they would be without their provider.

I relived all of my kills in just this fashion. I saw myself make the kill and then I felt its horrible results.

While in Southeast Asia I had seen women and children murdered, entire villages destroyed, for no reason or for the wrong reasons. I had not been involved in these killings, but now I had to experience them again, from the point of view not of the executor, but the executed.

On one occasion, for example, I was sent to a country bordering Vietnam to assassinate a government official who did not share the "American point of view." I went in with a team. Our goal was to eliminate this man at a small rural hotel where he was staying. This would make the unspoken statement that no one was out of reach of the United States government.

We sat in the jungle for four days, waiting for a clear shot at this official, but he was always surrounded by an entourage of bodyguards and secretaries. Finally, we gave up and decided on another tack: Late at night, when everyone was asleep, we would simply plant explosives and blow up the hotel.

That is exactly what we did. We surrounded the hotel with plastic explosives and leveled it at sunrise, killing the official along with about fifty people who were staying there. At the time I laughed about it and told my control officer that all the people deserved to die because they were guilty by association.

I saw this incident again during my near-death experience, but this time, I was hit by a rush of emotions and information. I felt the stark horror that all of those people felt as they realized their lives were being snuffed out. I experienced the pain their families felt when they discovered that they had lost loved ones in such a tragic way. In many cases I even felt the loss their absence would make to future generations.

All in all I contributed to the deaths of dozens of people in Southeast Asia, and reliving them was hard to take. The one saving grace was that at the time, I thought what I was doing was right. I was killing in the name of patriotism, which took the edge off the horrors I had committed.

When I returned to the United States after my military duty, I continued to work for the government, performing clandestine operations. This largely involved the transport of weapons to people and countries friendly to the United States. Sometimes I was even called upon to train these people in the fine art of sniping or demolition.

Now, in the life review, I was forced to see the death and destruction that had taken place in the world as a result of my actions. "We are all a link in the great chain of humanity," said the Being. "What you do has an effect on the other links in that chain."

Many examples of this came to mind, but one in particular stands out. I saw myself unloading weapons in a Central American country. They were to be used to fight a war that was supported by our country against the Soviet Union.

My task was simply to transfer these weapons from an airplane to our military interests in the area. When this transfer was completed, I got back on the airplane and left.

But leaving wasn't so easy in my life review. I stayed with the weapons and watched as they were distributed at a military staging area. Then I went with the guns as they were used in the job of killing, some of them murdering innocent people and some the not so innocent. All in all it was horrible to witness the results of my role in this war.

This weapons transfer in Central America was the last job I was involved in before being struck by lightning. I remember watching children cry because they had been told that their fathers were dead, and I knew these deaths were caused by the guns I had delivered.

Then that was it, the review was over.

When I finished the review, I arrived at a point of reflection in which I was able to look back on what I had just witnessed and come to a conclusion. I was ashamed. I realized I had led a very selfish life, rarely reaching out to help anyone. Almost never had I smiled as an act of brotherly love or just handed somebody a dollar because he was down and needed a boost. No, my life had been for me and me alone. I hadn't given a damn about my fellow humans.

I looked at the Being of Light and felt a deep sense of sorrow and shame. I expected a rebuke, some kind of cosmic shaking of my soul. I had reviewed my life and what I had seen was a truly worthless person. What did I deserve if not a rebuke?

As I gazed at the Being of Light I felt as though he was touching me. From that contact I felt a love and joy that could only be compared to the nonjudgmental compassion that a grandfather has for a grandchild. "Who you are is the difference that God makes," said the Being. "And that difference is love." There were no actual words spoken, but this thought was communicated to me through some form of telepathy. To this day, I am not sure of the exact meaning of this cryptic phrase. That is what was said, however.

Again I was allowed a period of reflection. How much love had I given people? How much love had I taken from them? From the review I had just had, I could see that for every good event in my life, there were twenty bad ones to weigh against it. If guilt were fat, I would have weighed five hundred pounds.

As the Being of Light moved away, I felt the burden of this guilt being removed. I had felt the pain and anguish of reflection, but from that I had gained the knowledge that I could use to correct my life. I could hear the Being's message in my head, again as if through telepathy: "Humans are powerful spiritual beings meant to create good on the earth. This good isn't usually accomplished in bold actions, but in singular acts of kindness between people. It's the little things that count, be-cause they are more spontaneous and show who you truly are."

I was elated. I now knew the simple secret to improving mankind. The amount of love and good feelings you have at the end of your life is equal to the love and good feelings you put out during your life. It was just that simple.

"My life will be better now that I have the secret," I said to the Being of Light.

It was then that I realized that I wouldn't be going back. I had no more life to live. I had been struck by lightning. I was dead.

3

"He's Dead"

I later learned that the scene in the ambulance was chaotic. The radio chatter with the hospital continued against the backdrop of Sandy's sobs. The medical technician continued his heroic efforts despite the reading on the heart monitor that showed me to be a flatliner. The ambulance driver kept the pedal to the floor and the lights flashing because that's what he did whether the passenger was dead or alive.

Doctors and nurses met the ambulance at the emergency-room door. The emergency medical team pulled me from the ambulance and wheeled me into the emergency room. With the efficient teamwork of people who have done the same job hundreds of times, the doctors and nurses began resuscitation efforts on my body. One doctor crawled onto the gurney and began pushing on my chest while a nurse put a plastic tube down my throat and began breathing into it. Another doctor stuck a long needle deep into my chest and injected a syringeful of Adrenalin.

Still there was no response.

The doctors continued to try. Electrical paddles were pressed to my chest to try and shock my heart back to life. More heart massage popped and cracked my ribs. "Come on, Dannion, come on!" one nurse shouted in my ear.

Nothing happened. The heart monitor was still flat, and there wasn't a twitch in my entire body.

"He didn't make it," said the attending physician. He pulled a sheet over my face and walked out of the room to sit down. A nurse called the morgue and then rolled me out into a hallway next to an elevator. There I would stay until the morgue attendants came up from the basement for my body.

With exhaustion and disappointment on his face, the attending physician went into the waiting room to tell Sandy and Tom what they already knew. "He didn't make it," he said. Both Sandy and Tom began to cry.

I didn't see any of this. I heard about it later from Tom. As the doctor said, I was dead.

4

The Crystal City

W hat happens now that I'm dead? I wondered. Where am I going?

I stared at the beautiful Being of Light who shimmered before me. He was like a bagful of diamonds emitting a soothing light of love. Any fear I might have had at the notion of being dead was quelled by the love that poured from the Being before me. His forgiveness was remarkable. Despite the horribly flawed life we had just witnessed, deep and meaningful forgiveness came to me from this Being. Rather than issuing harsh judgment, the Being of Light was a friendly counsel, letting me feel for myself the pain and the pleasure I had caused others. Instead of feeling shame and anguish, I was bathed in the love that embraced me through the light, and had to give nothing in return.

But I was dead. What would happen now? I put my trust in the Being of Light.

We began to move upward. I could hear a hum as my body began to vibrate at a higher rate of speed. We moved up from one level to the next, like an airplane climbing gently into the sky. We were surrounded by a shimmering mist, cool and thick like fog off the ocean.

Around us I could see energy fields that looked like prisms of light. Some of this energy flowed like great rivers, while some eddied like tiny streams. I even saw lakes and small pools of it. (Up close these were clearly fields of energy, but from a distance, they resembled rivers and lakes the way you would see them from an airplane.)

Through the mist I could see mountains the color of deep-blue velvet. There were no sharp peaks and craggy slopes with jagged edges in this mountain range. The mountains were gentle, with rounded peaks and lush crevices that were a deeper blue.

On the mountainside were lights. Through the mist they looked like houses turning on their lights at twilight. There were many such lights, and I could tell by the way we swooped down and accelerated that we were headed directly for them. At first we moved toward the right side of this mountain range, which was enormous. Then we banked left and moved swiftly toward the shorter side.

How am I moving? I wondered, looking around at the heavenly landscape beneath us. We were floating the way I always imagined angels do, just lifting off the ground and flying. Then my thinking took a philosophical turn. Am I really moving or is this just a journey inside my dead body? Before we landed I continued to ask the Being where I was and how I had gotten there, but he offered no response. When I pushed for answers I got none, but I wasn't dissatisfied. As I thought hard, the Being swelled and provided comfort in his might. Even without the answers I wanted so desperately, I felt at ease because of the power that pulsed around me. Wherever I am, there is nothing here that can hurt me, I told myself. I relaxed in the presence of the Being.

Like wingless birds, we swept into a city of cathedrals. These cathedrals were made entirely of a crystalline substance that glowed with a light that shone powerfully from within. We stood before one. I felt small and insignificant next to this architectural masterpiece. Clearly this had been built by angels to show the grandeur of God, I thought. It had spires as high and pointed as those of the great cathedrals of France, and walls as massive and powerful as those of the Mormon Tabernacle in Salt Lake City. The walls were made of large glass bricks that glowed from within. These structures were not related to a specific religion of any kind. They were a monument to the glory of God.

I was awestruck. This place had a power that seemed to pulsate through the air. I knew that I was in a place of learning. I wasn't there to witness my life or to see what value it had had, I was there to be instructed. I looked to the Being of Light and thought a question: Is this heaven? I received no answer. Instead we moved forward, up a splendid walk and through glowing portals of crystal.

When we entered the structure, the Being of Light was with me no more. I looked around for him and saw no one. Rows of benches were lined up across the room, and that radiant light made everything glow and feel like love. I sat on one of the benches and looked around the room for my spiritual guide. Sitting alone in this strange and glorious place made me somewhat uncomfortable. There was no one to be seen, yet I had a strong feeling that the benches were filled with people just like me, spirit beings who were here for the first time and were puzzled by what they were seeing. I looked around again, first to my left and then to my right, but still saw nobody. There are beings here, I said to myself. I know there are. I continued to look around, but still no one materialized.

This place reminded me of a magnificent lecture hall. The benches were positioned in such a way that whoever was sitting on them would face a long podium that glowed like white quartz. The wall behind this podium was a spectacular carousel of colors, ranging from pastels to bright neons. Its beauty was hypnotic. I watched the colors blend and merge, surging and pulsing the way the ocean does when you are far out at sea and look into its depths.

I was certain there were new spirits surrounding me, but now I knew why they couldn't be seen. If we could see one another, we wouldn't be giving our full attention to the podium at the front of the room. Something is going to happen up there, I thought.

In the next moment the space behind the podium was filled with Beings of Light. They faced the benches where I was sitting and radiated a glow that was both kindly and wise.

I sat back on the bench and waited. What happened next was the most amazing part of my spiritual journey.

5

The Boxes of Knowledge

I was able to count the Beings as they stood behind the podium. There were thirteen of them, standing shoulder to shoulder and stretched across the stage. I was aware of other things about them, too, probably through some form of telepathy. Each one of them represented a different emotional and psychological characteristic that all humans have. For example, one of these Beings was intense and passionate, while another was artistic and emotional. One was bold and energetic, yet another possessive and loyal. In human terms, it was as though each one represented a different sign of the zodiac. In spiritual terms, these Beings went far beyond the signs of the zodiac. They emanated these emotions in such a way that I could feel them.

Now more than ever I knew that this was a place of learning. I would be steeped in knowledge, taught in a way that I had never been taught before. There would be no books and no memorization. In the presence of these Beings of Light, I would become knowledge and know everything that was important to know. I could ask any question and know the answer. It was like being a drop of water bathed in the knowledge of the ocean, or a beam of light knowing what all light knows.

I had only to think a question to explore the essence of the answer. In a split second I understood how light works, the ways in which spirit is incorporated into the physical life, why it is possible for people to think and act in so many different ways. Ask and you shall perceive, is the way I sum it up.

These Beings of Light were different from the one that met me when I first died. They had the same silver-blue glow of that first Being, but with light that glowed deep blue from within them. This color carried with it a great sense of might and seemed to draw from the same source that traits like heroism come from. I have never seen the color since then, but it seemed to signify that these Beings were among the greatest of their kind. I felt as awestruck and proud to be in their presence as I would to be standing with Joan of Arc or George Washington.

The Beings came at me one at a time. As each one approached, a box the size of a videotape came from its chest and zoomed right at my face.

The first time this happened I flinched, thinking I was going to be hit. But a moment before impact, the box opened to reveal what appeared to be a tiny television picture of a world event that was yet to happen. As I watched, I felt myself drawn right into the picture, where I was able to live the event. This happened twelve times, and twelve times I stood in the midst of many events that would shake the world in the future.

At the time I didn't know these were future events. All I knew was that I was seeing things of great significance and that they were coming to me as clearly as the nightly news, with one great difference: I was being pulled into the screen.

Much later, when I returned to life, I wrote down 117 events that I witnessed in the boxes. For three years nothing happened. Then in 1978, events that I had seen in the boxes began to come true. In the eighteen years since I died and went to this place, ninety-five of these events have taken place.

On this day, September 17, 1975, the future came to me a box at a time.

BOXES ONE THROUGH THREE:
VISIONS OF A DEMORALIZED COUNTRY

Boxes one, two, and three showed the mood of America in the aftermath of the war in Southeast Asia. They revealed scenes of spiritual loss in our country that were byproducts of that war, which weakened the structure of America and eventually the world.

The scenes were of prisoners of war, weak and wasted from hunger, as they waited in the rugged prisons of North Vietnam for American ambassadors to come and free them. I could feel their fear and then despair when they realized one by one that no help would be forthcoming and that they would live out their remaining years as slaves in jungle prisons. These were the MIAs, those military men considered "missing in action."

The MIAs were already an issue in 1975, but they were used as a starting point in the visions to show an America that was slipping into spiritual decline.

I could see America falling into enormous debt. This came to me as scenes of money going out of a room much faster than it was coming in. Through some kind of telepathy I was aware that this money represented the increase in the national debt and that it spelled danger down the road. I also saw people waiting in long lines for the basics of life like clothing and food.

Many scenes of spiritual hunger came from the first two boxes as well. I saw people who were transparent in such a way as to reveal that they were hollow. This hollowness, it was explained to me telepathically, was caused by a loss of faith in America and what it stood for. The war in Southeast Asia had combined with inflation and distrust in our government to create a spiritual void. This void was added to by our loss of love for God.

This spiritual depravity resulted in a number of shocking visions: people rioting and looting because they wanted more material goods than they had, kids shooting other kids with high-powered rifles, criminals stealing cars, young men firing on other young men from the windows of cars. Scenes like these played out in front of me like scenes from a gangster movie.

Most of the criminals were children or adolescents that no one cared about. As I watched image after image, it became painfully clear to me that these kids had no family units, and as a result, they were acting like wolves.

I was confused because I couldn't figure out how American

children could be left to roam and murder. Didn't they have parental guidance? I wondered. How could such a thing happen in our country?

In the third box I found myself facing the seal of the president of the United States. I don't know where I was, but I saw the initials "RR" emblazoned beneath this seal. Then I was standing in the midst of newspapers, looking at their editorial cartoons. One after the other I saw cartoons of a cowboy. He was riding the range or shooting down bad guys in saloons. This vision was festooned with satirical illustrations from around the country from such newspapers as *The Boston Globe,* the *Chicago Tribune,* and the *Los Angeles Times.* The dates on the newspapers ranged from 1983 to 1987, and it was clear from the nature of the drawings that they were about the president of the United States, who projected the image of being a cowboy to the rest of the world.

I could also tell that the man in these cartoons was an actor, because they all had a theatrical look to them. One of the cartoons even referred to "Butch Cassidy and the Sundance Kid" and played off the famous scene in that movie in which the two outlaws jump off a cliff into a shallow pool of water. Yet despite the vividness of the newspaper clippings, I was unable to see the face under the cowboy hat. I now know that "RR" stood for Ronald Reagan, but at the time I had no idea who the "cowboy" was. A few months later, when I was recalling these visions for Dr. Raymond Moody, the noted psychiatrist and researcher of near-death experiences, he asked me who I thought "RR" was. Without hesitation I said, "Robert Redford." He has never let me forget that mistake and ribs me about it every time we get together.

BOXES FOUR AND FIVE:
STRIFE AND HATRED IN THE HOLY LANDS

Boxes four and five were scenes from the Middle East, showing how this area of eternal strife would reach a boiling point. Religion would play a large role in these problems, as would the economy. A constant need for outside money fueled much of the anger and hatred that I saw in these boxes.

In the first of these boxes I saw two agreements taking place.

In the first, Israelis and Arabs were agreeing to something, but what was unclear to me.

The second accord was one that I could see in some detail. Men were shaking hands and there was much talk about a new country. Then I saw a collage of images: the River Jordan, a settlement from Israel that was spreading into Jordan, and a map on which the country of Jordan was changing color. As I watched this puzzling collage unfold, I heard a Being speak telepathically to me and say that the country of Jordan would exist no more. I did not hear the name of the new country.

This agreement was nothing more than a front by the Israelis to create a police force composed of Israelis and Arabs. This was a very harsh police force, cruel and unyielding. I saw them wearing blue-and-silver uniforms and having a tight grip on the people of this region. So tight was their grip, in fact, that world leaders became highly critical of Israel. Many collaborators on both sides kept an eye on their own people and reported their activities to this police force. They served to make everyone suspicious, causing trust in these societies to disappear.

I could see Israel becoming isolated from the rest of the

world. As things worsened, there were images of Israel preparing for war against other countries, including Russia and a Chinese-and-Arab consortium. Jerusalem was somehow at the eye of this conflict, but I am not sure exactly how. From newspaper headlines that appeared in the vision, I could see that some incident in that holy city had served to trigger this war.

These visions revealed Israel as being spiritually hollow. I had the sense of it being a country of strong government but weak morals. Image after image came of Israelis reacting with hatred toward Palestinians and other Arabs, and I was steeped in the sense that these people as a nation had forgotten God and were now driven by racial hatred.

The fifth box showed oil being used as a weapon to control the international economy. I saw images of Mecca and then of the Saudi people. While these images streamed before me, a telepathic voice said that oil production was being cut off to destroy America's economy and to milk money from the world economy. The price of oil was going up and up, said the voice, and Saudi Arabia was making an alliance with Syria and China. I could see Arab and Oriental people shaking hands and making deals. As these images came to me, I could sense money being given by the Saudis to Asian countries like North Korea, all in the hopes of destabilizing the economy of the Asian region.

I wondered where this alliance began, and I was able to see a close-up of Syrians and Chinese signing papers and shaking hands in a building that I knew was in Syria. The date that came to me was 1992.

Another date came to me—1993—and with it came images

of Syrian and Chinese scientists working in laboratories to develop a missile that could deliver chemical and biological weapons. Nuclear weapons were becoming things of the past, and these countries wanted to develop new weapons of destruction.

The boxes kept coming.

BOX SIX:
VISIONS OF NUCLEAR DESTRUCTION

Number six was terrifying. I was drawn into the box and found myself in a cool, forested area beside a river. Next to the river was a massive cement structure, square and foreboding. I was fearful and didn't know why. Suddenly the earth shook and the top of this cement structure exploded. I knew it was a nuclear explosion and could sense hundreds of people dying around me as it took place. The year 1986 was given to me through telepathy, as was the word *wormwood*. It wasn't until a decade later, when the Chernobyl nuclear plant exploded near Kiev in the Soviet Union, that I was able to associate these pictures with an event. It was then that I made another connection between the vision in this box and the nuclear disaster in the USSR. The word *Chernobyl* means "wormwood" in Russian.

A second nuclear accident appeared in the box, this in a northern sea so badly polluted that no ships would travel there. The water was a pale red and was covered with dead or dying fish. Around the water were peaks and valleys that made me think I was seeing a fjord like those in Norway. I couldn't tell where this was, but I knew that the world was frightened at what had happened, because radiation from this accident could spread everywhere and affect all of humankind. The date on the picture was 1995.

The vision didn't stop there. People were dying and deformed as a result of these nuclear catastrophes. In a series of what seemed like television pictures, I saw cancer victims and mutated babies in Russia, Norway, Sweden, and Finland, not hundreds or thousands of people, but tens of thousands, in a vast array of deformity, going on through generations. The poisons released by these accidents were carried to the rest of the world through water, which was tainted forever by this nuclear waste. The Being made it clear that humans had created a horrible power that had not been contained. By letting this power out of their control, the Soviets had destroyed their own country and possibly the world.

The box showed me the fear in people's hearts that resulted from these nuclear accidents. As the images of this fear unfolded, I somehow understood that environmentalism would emerge as the world's new religion. People would consider a clean environment a key to salvation more than they ever had before. Political parties would spring up around the issue of a cleaner planet, and political fortunes would be made or broken based upon feelings about the environment.

From Chernobyl and this second accident, I could see that the Soviet Union would wither and die, with the Soviet people losing faith in their government and the government losing its grip on the people.

The economy played a strong role in these visions. I saw people carrying bags of money into stores and coming out with small bags of goods. People with military uniforms wandered the streets in Soviet cities begging for food, some obviously starving to death. People ate rotted potatoes and apples, and crowds rioted to get at trucks filled with food.

The word *Georgia* appeared in a Cyrillic script, and I could see a mafia developing in Moscow that I assume came from the state of Georgia in the Soviet Union. This mafia was a growing power that was in competition with the Soviet government. In scene after scene, I saw mafia members operating freely in a city that I think was Moscow.

I felt no joy as I watched the Soviet Union collapse. Although Soviet-style communism was dying right before my eyes, the Being of Light was saying that this was a cautious moment instead of a glorious one. "Watch the Soviet Union," he said. "How the Russian people go, so goes the world. What happens to Russia is the basis for everything that will happen to the economy of the free world."

BOX SEVEN:
THE ENVIRONMENTAL RELIGION

The seventh box held powerful images of environmental destruction. I could see areas of the world radiating energy, glowing like a radium watch face in the dark. Telepathically I could hear voices speaking of the need to clean up the environment.

These voices came out of Russia at first, but then the accents changed and I could tell that they were emanating from South America, probably from Uruguay or Paraguay.

I saw the speaker from Russia as he talked with zeal about our need to heal the environment. People rallied around him quickly, and he soon became so powerful that he was elected one of the leaders of the United Nations. I saw this Russian riding on a white horse, and I knew that his rise would come before the year 2000.

BOXES EIGHT AND NINE:
CHINA BATTLES RUSSIA

In boxes eight and nine were visions of China's growing anger toward the Soviet Union. When these visions took place in 1975, I didn't know that the Soviet Union would break up. Now I think the tension I saw in that vision was a result of the death of Soviet communism, which left the Chinese the leaders of the Communist world.

At the time, the visions were a puzzle to me. I saw border disputes and heavy fighting between Soviet and Chinese armies. Finally, the Chinese amassed their armies at the border and pushed into the region.

The main battle was over a railroad, which the Chinese took in heavy fighting. They then pushed deep into the Soviet Union, cutting the country in half and taking over the oil fields of Siberia. I saw snow, blood, and oil and knew that the loss of life had been heavy.

BOXES TEN AND ELEVEN:
ECONOMIC EARTHQUAKES, DESERT STORM

Boxes ten and eleven came in rapid succession. They revealed scenes of the economic collapse of the world. In general terms, these visions showed a world in horrible turmoil by the turn of the century, one that resulted in a new world order that was truly one of feudalism and strife.

In one of the visions, people lined up to take money out of

banks. In another the banks were being closed by the government. The voice that accompanied the visions told me that this would take place in the nineties and would be the beginning of an economic strife that would lead to the bankruptcy of America by the year 2000.

The box showed images of dollar signs flying by as people pumped gas and looked distressed. I knew this meant that oil prices were accelerating out of control.

I saw thirteen new nations entering the world market in the late nineties. These were nations with manufacturing capabilities that put them on a competitive footing with the United States. One by one our European markets began to give their business to these countries, which slowed our economy even more. All of this led to a greatly weakened economy.

But the end of America as a world power came as visions of two horrendous earthquakes in which buildings were swaying and toppling over like a child's wooden blocks. I knew that these quakes happened sometime before the end of the century, but I couldn't tell where they took place. I do remember seeing a large body of water that was probably a river.

The cost of rebuilding these destroyed cities would be the final straw for our government, now so financially broken that it would hardly be able to keep itself alive. The voice in the vision told me that it would be this way while the images from the box showed Americans starving and lined up for food.

At the tail end of box ten came images of warfare in the desert, a massive show of military might. I saw armies racing toward one another in the desert, with great clouds of dust billowing from the treads of tanks as they crossed the barren ground. There was cannon fire and explosions that looked like lightning. The earth shook and then there was silence. Like a bird, I flew over acres of destroyed army equipment.

As I left the box, the date 1990 came into my head. That was the year of Desert Storm, the military operation that squashed the army of Iraq for occupying Kuwait.

Box eleven began with Iran and Iraq in possession of nuclear and chemical weapons. Included in this arsenal was a submarine loaded with nuclear missiles. The year, said a voice in the vision, was 1993.

I saw this submarine powering through the waters of the Middle East, piloted by people I knew to be Iranians. I could tell that their purpose was to stop the shipping of oil from the Middle East. They were so praiseful of God in their speech that I had the sense that this was some kind of religious mission.

The missiles that occupied the desert of the Middle East were equipped with chemical warheads. I don't know where they were aimed, but I do know that there was worldwide fear of the intentions of the Arab nations that had them.

Chemical warfare played a role in a horrible vision of terrorism that takes place in France before 2000. It begins when the French publish a book that infuriates the Arab world. I don't know the title of this book, but the result of its publication is a chemical attack by Arabs on a city in France. A chemical is put into the water supply, and thousands drink it and die before it can be eliminated.

In one brief vision I saw Egyptians rioting in the streets while a voice told me that by 1997, Egypt would collapse as a democracy and be taken over by religious fanatics.

The final visions from box eleven were like many images we now see of Sarajavo: modern cities crumbling beneath the weight of warfare, their inhabitants fighting one another for reasons ranging from racism to religious conflict. I saw many towns worldwide where desperate citizens were eating their own dead.

In one such scene, Europeans in a hilly region of the world were weeping as they cooked human meat. In rapid succession I saw people of all five races eating their fellow humans.

BOX TWELVE:
TECHNOLOGY AND VIRUS

The eleventh box was gone and I was into the twelfth box. Its visions addressed an important event in the distant future, the decade of the nineties (remember, this was 1975), when many of the great changes would take place.

In this box I watched as a biological engineer from the Middle East found a way to alter DNA and create a biological virus that would be used in the manufacture of computer chips. This discovery allowed for huge strides in science and technology. Japan, China, and other countries of the Pacific Rim experienced boom times as a result of this discovery and became powers of incredible magnitude. Computer chips produced from this process found their way into virtually every form of technology, from cars and airplanes to vacuum cleaners and blenders.

Before the turn of the century, this man was among the richest in the world, so rich that he had a stranglehold on the world economy. Still the world welcomed him, since the computer chips he had designed somehow put the world on an even keel.

Gradually he succumbed to his own power. He began to

think of himself as a deity and insisted on greater control of the world. With that extra control, he began to rule the world.

His method of rule was unique. Everyone in the world was mandated by law to have one of his computer chips inserted underneath his or her skin. This chip contained all of an individual's personal information. If a government agency wanted to know something, all it had to do was scan your chip with a special device. By doing so, it could discover everything about you, from where you worked and lived to your medical records and even what kind of illnesses you might get in the future.

There was an even more sinister side to this chip. A person's lifetime could be limited by programming this chip to dissolve and kill him with the viral substance it was made from. Lifetimes were controlled like this to avoid the cost that growing old places on the government. It was also used as a means of eliminating people with chronic illnesses that put a drain on the medical system.

People who refused to have chips implanted in their bodies roamed as outcasts. They could not be employed and were denied government services.

THE FINAL VISIONS

At the very end came a thirteenth vision. I don't know where it came from. I didn't see a Being of Light bring it forward in a box, nor did I see one take it away. This vision was in many ways the most important of all because it summed up everything I had seen in the twelve boxes. Through telepathy I could hear a Being say, "If you follow what you have been taught and keep living the same way you have lived the last thirty years, all of this will surely be upon you. If you change, you can avoid the coming war."

Scenes from a horrible world war accompanied this message. As the visions appeared on the screen, the Being told me that the years 1994 through 1996 were critical ones in determining whether this war would break out. "If you follow this dogma, the world by the year 2004 will not be the same one you now know," said the Being. "But it can still be changed and you can help change it."

Scenes from World War III came to life before me. I was in a hundred places at once, from deserts to forests, and saw a world filled with fighting and chaos. Somehow it was clear that this final war, an Armaggedon if you will, was caused by fear. In one of the most puzzling visions of all, I saw an army of women in black robes and veils marching through a European city.

"The fear these people are feeling is an unnecessary one," said the Being of Light. "But it is a fear so great that humans will give up all freedoms in the name of safety."

I also saw scenes that were not of war, including many visions of natural disasters. In parts of the world that had once been fertile with wheat and corn, I saw parched desert and furrowed fields that farmers had given up on. In other parts of the world, torrential rainstorms had gouged out the earth, eating away topsoil and creating rivers of thick, dark mud.

People were starving in this vision. They were begging for food on the streets, holding out bowls and cups and even their hands in hopes that someone or something would offer them a scrap to eat. In some of the pictures, people had given up or were too weak to beg and were curled on the ground waiting for the gift of death.

I saw civil wars breaking out in Central and South America and the rise of socialist governments in all of these countries before the year 2000. As these wars intensified, millions of refugees streamed across the U.S. border, looking for a new life in North America. Nothing we did could stop these immigrants. They were driven by fear of death and loss of confidence in God.

I saw millions of people streaming north out of El Salvador and Nicaragua, and more millions crossing the Rio Grande into Texas. There were so many of them that we had to line the border with troops and force them back across the river.

The Mexican economy was broken by these refugees and collapsed under the strain.

A s these visions ended, I had the amazing realization that these Beings were desperately trying to help us, not because we were such good guys, but because without us advancing spiritually here on earth, they could not become successful in their world. "You humans are truly the heroes," a Being told me. "Those who go to earth are heroes and heroines, because you are doing something that no other spiritual beings have the courage to do. You have gone to earth to co-create with God."

A s I was presented with each of these boxes, my mind pondered the same questions, over and over: Why is this happening to me? What are these scenes in the boxes and why are they being shown to me? I didn't know what was going on, and despite the seemingly infinite knowledge that I had been given earlier, I was unable to find the answers to those questions. I was seeing the future and I didn't know why.

After the final visions, the thirteenth Being of Light answered my questions. He was more powerful than the others, or at least I assume he was. His colors were more intense, and the other Beings seemed to defer to him. His personality was conveyed in his light and encompassed the emotions of his fellow Beings.

Without words, he told me that everything I had just seen was in the future, but not necessarily cast in stone. "The flow of human events can be changed, but first people have to know what they are," said the Being. He communicated to me again their belief that humans were great, powerful, and mighty spiritual Beings. "We here see everyone who goes to the earth as great adventurers," he said. "You had the courage to go and expand your life and take your place in the great adventure that God created known as the world."

He then told me my purpose on earth. "You are there to create spiritualistic capitalism," he said. "You are to engage this coming system by changing people's thought processes. Show people how to rely on their spiritual selves instead of the government and churches. Religion is fine, but don't let people be entirely controlled by it. Humans are mighty spiritual beings. All they need to realize is that love is treating others the way they themselves want to be treated."

Then the Being let me know what I was supposed to do back on earth. I was to create centers where people could come to reduce stress in their lives. Through this reduction of stress, said the Being, humans would come to realize, "as we do," that they are higher spiritual beings. They would become less fearful and more loving of their fellow man.

I then saw a vision of seven rooms, each a step in the process:

- a "therapy room," in which people come together and talk to each other
- a massage clinic, where people are not only massaged, but they massage others
- a sensory-deprivation chamber, which is some kind of chamber that allows people to relax and go deep within themselves
- a room equipped with biofeedback machines that lets people see the extent to which they can control their emotions
- an area for readings that allows those with psychic abilities to provide patients with personal insights
- a room with a bed whose musical components relax a person so deeply that he can actually leave his body
- a reflection chamber made of polished steel or copper on the inside and shaped in such a way that the person inside can't see his own reflection. (I envisioned the walls as being made of polished stainless steel, but I didn't understand the purpose of this chamber.)

An eighth component of the process is when the person goes back to the room with the bed and he is once again connected to the biofeedback instruments. As the person enters a deep stage of relaxation, he is guided to a spiritual realm. The biofeedback instruments help him realize the feelings required to reach those states of deep relaxation.

"The purpose of all of these rooms is to show people that they can be in control of their lives through God," said the Being.

I now know that each of these rooms represents a modern form of an ancient oracle, the temples of spirit and mystery that were popular in ancient Greece. For instance, what takes place in the bed is similar to the dream incubation that took place in the temples of Asklepios. The reading area represents the temple of Delphi, where people used to talk to spirits. The reflection chamber is the "necromanteum" of Ephyra, where the ancients went to see apparitions of their departed loved ones. (I didn't discover this until many years later, when Dr. Raymond Moody, who has a doctorate in philosophy as well as an M.D., noticed a relationship between these rooms and the oracles.)

How was I supposed to build these modern-day oracles? I was told by the Being not to worry, that the components for all of these rooms would come to me, and as they came to me, I would put them in place. How can this be? I thought. I don't know anything about this stuff. I know a little about meditation because I used to do that when I took karate as a kid. But I certainly don't know enough about these things to build this kind of facility. "Don't worry," said the Being. "It will come to you."

The Being called these places "centers." He told me that it would be my mission on earth to create them. Then he told me it was time to go back to earth.

I resisted the return. I liked this place. I had been there so little time, but already I could see that I was free to roam in so many directions that it was like having total access to the universe. After coming here, going back to earth would be as confining as living on the head of a pin. Still, I was given no choice.

"This we ask of you. You must return to fulfill this mission," said the Being of Light.

And then I came back.

6
Coming Back

I left the Crystal City by fading into an atmosphere that was a rich blue-gray color. This was the same place I had gone when I was first struck by lightning, so I can only assume that it was the barrier we cross when we enter the spirit world.

I came out of this atmosphere on my back. Slowly, and without effort, I was able to roll over, and when I did, I could see that I was floating above a hallway. Below me was a gurney with a body on it, covered with a sheet and lying still. The person underneath the sheet was dead.

Around the corner and down the hall I heard an elevator open. I saw two orderlies in white outfits emerge from the elevator and walk toward the dead man. They were talking like two guys who had just left a pool hall, and one of them was smoking, blowing clouds of smoke toward the ceiling where I was hovering. I sensed that they were there to take the body to the morgue.

Before they reached the dead man, my buddy Tommy came through the door and stationed himself next to the gurney. It was then that I realized that the man underneath the sheet was me. I was dead. It was me—or what was left of me—who was about to be rolled off to the morgue!

I could feel Tommy's sadness that I was gone. He couldn't let me go. As he stood there and stared at my body, I felt the love coming from him as he begged me to come back to life.

By now, my entire family had arrived at the hospital, and I could feel their prayers, too. My parents, brother, and sister were sitting in the waiting room with Sandy. They didn't know I was dead because the doctor didn't have the heart to tell them. Instead, he said that I probably wasn't going to last much longer.

Love truly can give life, I thought, as I hovered in the hallway. Love can make the difference. As I focused on Tommy, I felt myself become denser. In the next instant, I was looking up at the sheet.

This return to my human body put me in possession of its pain. I was on fire again, aching with the agony of being burned from the inside out, as though acid was in all of my cells. A ringing started in my ears that was so loud I thought I was inside a bell tower. My tongue had swelled and filled my mouth completely. On my body were blue lines crisscrossing me, marking the path the lightning had taken as it surged from my head to the floor. I couldn't see them, but I could feel their burn.

I couldn't move, which is a bad state to be in when orderlies are coming to take you to the morgue. I tried to move, but no matter how hard I tried, I couldn't twitch a muscle. Finally, I did the only thing I could. I blew on the sheet.

"He's alive, he's alive!" shouted Tommy.

"Look, yeah," said one of the orderlies. He pulled back the sheet and there I was, my tongue lolling out of my mouth and my eyes rolling around. Suddenly I began to convulse like an epileptic having a grand mal seizure.

The orderly who was smoking threw his cigarette to the floor and pushed me back into the emergency room. "He's still alive," he shouted. The doctors and nurses sprang into action.

They worked on me for another thirty minutes. One doctor shouted orders, and the nurses followed them. In rapid succession they stuck needles in my arms, my neck, and my heart. Someone put the paddles back onto my chest, but I don't remember feeling any electricity, so perhaps they were just trying to monitor my heart rate. Someone stuck something into my mouth. Someone else held my eyes open and looked at them with a flashlight. Through all of this, I wished I were dead and back in the Crystal City, where there was no pain and knowledge flowed freely.

But I couldn't go back. As the medicines worked their magic, I began to feel as though I was really in the room. I couldn't see well, and the bright lights over my head burned my eyes so badly that I cried out to have them turned off. But I was back in the real world to stay.

When they were finished in emergency, I was rolled into a

small side room. This room had a curtain on it instead of a door and was apparently used when patients were ready to be transferred from the emergency room to the intensive care unit.

The doctor gave me a shot of morphine and I was suddenly hovering above my body again, looking down as Tommy snuck into the room to be at my side. I watched as he looked through the drawers and cabinets, relying on his Navy medical training to determine the kind of work that was done in this room.

Several days later, in slow, almost incoherent, speech, I told Tommy some of what had happened. Then I said, "I saw you rummaging through the shelves and drawers in that room. What were you doing?" Since I had been unconscious from morphine at the time, it shocked him that I was able to see what he had done, and convinced him that something truly extraordinary had occurred when I died.

But that came later. For the first seven days I was paralyzed. People sat with me in my room, but I couldn't embrace them. Friends and family spoke to me, but I could return only a few words. Sometimes I was aware of people being in the room, but I didn't know who they were or why they were there. Sometimes I wasn't even aware that those things in the room were people. And since light hurt my eyes so badly, I needed to have the room darkened with blackout curtains.

The world I lived in when I was asleep was the one that made sense. If my waking world could be considered "incoherent," as one doctor put it, then my dream time was a model of coherency. When I was asleep, I was back in the Crystal City, being trained to do the many things that the vision would require me to do. As I slept I was led to understand electronic circuitry and to recognize the components I would need to make the bed.

These dreams went on for several hours each day, for at least twenty days. They were wonderful. My waking world was filled with pain and irritation. My sleeping world was filled with freedom, knowledge, and excitement. Awake, the people around me were only waiting for me to die. Asleep, I was being shown how to live a fruitful life.

When I say that the people in the hospital were only waiting for me to die, I'm not being cynical. They never expected me to make it, and they considered me a sort of medical mystery.

For instance, a team of specialists came from New York City just to examine me. One of them told me that no one in his memory had survived such a jolt of lightning and that he wanted to examine me while I was still alive. They spent three days at the hospital, poking and prodding me as I lay paralyzed. One particularly horrible thing they did was a pincushion test in which they stuck seven-inch-long needles into my legs to see if I could feel anything. The amazing thing was that I couldn't feel the needles at all, even though I saw them being inserted into my legs.

I was terrified. I must have looked very frightened when they started the pincushion test, because the doctor stopped just before inserting the needle into my leg and looked up at me. I don't think he realized that I knew what was going on. He stood there with rubber gloves on and the needle in his hand and he said, "We're going to look for any nerve that is alive in there." He then slipped the needle right into my leg.

I could see the look of surprise on the faces of the doctors and nurses every time they came into the room and found me still alive. I know they expected my heart to give out or the pain to kill me, and to tell you the truth, the pain was so great that I wanted to die. But I also knew the truth: I was going to survive. My experience in the Crystal City and the dreams I was having every night assured me that I was doomed to live.

And the word "doomed" was an accurate description of how I felt about going on. I was in constant agony now. I have often wondered why I couldn't feel the pincushion test. I have come to the conclusion that the pain inside my body was so great that I couldn't feel anything that was being done to it from the outside. After all, how painful can needle sticks be to a person who is burned from the inside out? The pain was so overwhelming, and I was in such bad shape, that I couldn't imagine healing enough to have a normal life. That is why I felt doomed to be alive.

After eight days flat on my back, I made a discovery. I could move my left hand.

I discovered this when my nose began to itch. The pain had subsided, and now I had itchy spots all over me that felt like hives. One of the worst areas was my nose. I had become so accustomed to being paralyzed that I would just lie there and hope that the itching would go away. It didn't. I began to think about scratching my nose when I realized the fingers of my left hand were moving. With great concentration I began to pull my hand up toward my face. The effort was like lifting a heavy barbell. Several times, I had to stop and rest from the exertion. Finally, after what surely must have been an hour, I reached my nose. The spot was no longer itchy, but I scratched it anyway for victory's sake. That was when I saw that my fingernails had been burned off by the lightning and were nothing but black stubs.

It was time to begin my own rehabilitation.

I had decided to make my body work again, one muscle at a time. My brother brought a copy of *Gray's Anatomy* to the hospital. This book describes the workings of the human body, with detailed written explanations and a line drawing of each body part. My brother made me a headdress out of a coat hanger and a pencil so I could turn the pages with the eraser on the pencil by moving my head.

I started looking at every muscle in my hand, examining the picture in the book while I focused on the muscles and tried to move them one at a time. Hour after hour, I stared at *Gray's Anatomy* and then stared at my hand, talking to it, cursing at it, making it move. When the left hand worked, I did the same thing with the right hand, and so on down my entire body. The greatest moments came when I was able to move a muscle, even as little as an eighth of an inch. When that happened, I knew my body was going to work again.

A few days after starting this form of therapy, I decided to get out of bed. I had no hope of walking, at least not yet. All I wanted to do was get out of bed and then get back in under my own power.

Late at night, when no nurses were in the room, I rolled out of bed and hit the floor with a sickening thud. Then I struggled to get back into the bed I had just bailed out of. I rolled onto my belly and inched my rear end into the air like a worm. Then I grabbed at the bed's iron bars, the sheets, the mattress, and anything else I could get a palsied grip on. Several times I fell back to the cold floor. Once I fell asleep from exhaustion. But by morning, I was back in bed.

Since the nurses checked the patients every four hours, I figured the climb back had taken me at least that long. I was as happy and exhausted as a climber who has made it to the top of Mount Everest. I knew I was on the way back.

Still, no one else thought I was going to make it. The nurses had looks of despair when they came in to see me. I heard doctors in the hallway say that my heart was too far gone and that I was going to die. Even my family had its doubts. They saw me laboring for breath and struggling to move, and they thought it would be only a short time before I was dead. "Oh Dannion, you look very good today," my folks would say, but the look on their faces was one of utter horror, as if they were examining a cat squashed in their driveway.

I wish I had had a movie camera positioned by my head, to record the people's expressions as they tried to maintain their composure when they saw me.

One day, for example, my aunt came into the room and stood at the foot of the bed. She stared for a minute, until she was joined by her daughter, who stood next to her.

"He looks like Jesus, doesn't he?" said my aunt.

"He does," said my cousin. "He has sort of a glow, like Jesus must have had when they took him down from the cross."

Another time, a neighbor came to visit. He entered the room with a big smile on his face, but when he stood over me and looked down, the smile wilted in direct proportion to the pain he must have been feeling in his stomach. The sight of me was making him sick.

"Don't throw up on me," I said.

Thankfully, he backed up and left the room.

One time a visitor did throw up. I was awakened by someone pulling back my curtain and saying, "Oh my God!" Then
they just lost it. They bent over and heaved and continued to
heave as they backed out of the room. No one has admitted to
doing this, and I still don't know who it was.

Throughout this horror show I continued to commune with
the Beings of Light. Night after night my dreams showed me
my future. I was shown circuitry, building plans, and component parts. I was also given a deadline: I was to have the
working model of the center completed by 1992.

By the end of September 1975 I was released from the
hospital. Against all odds I had survived. The doctors also
thought that I would be blinded by the experience, but they
were wrong. My eyes had become so sensitive to the light that
I had to wear welder's goggles outside, but I could still see.
None of the doctors thought I would be able to move again,
but now, only thirteen days after being struck by lightning, I
was able to crawl out of bed and drop into a wheelchair. It took
me nearly thirty minutes to do it, but I insisted on doing it
myself. They also predicted that my heart would stop within a
few hours of the lightning strike. But here it was, still beating
as they rolled me down the hall and out to the car.

Before I left, one of the doctors asked me what this experience had been like. I was slow to respond, but the image that
came immediately to mind was that of Joan of Arc.

"I feel like God burned me at the stake," I said in a stum-
bling speech.

Then I was wheeled out of the hospital and into a waiting car.

7

At Home

I know that Sandy picked me up at the hospital because she told me later that she had. I imagine there was some kind of fanfare when I got home, but I honestly don't remember any balloons or signs that said "Welcome Home, Danny." I didn't hear anyone say that I had been sent home to die, but that is what the doctors told my parents and Sandy. "Let him go home and live out his last days," said one of the doctors. "He'll be more comfortable there."

The truth was that most of the time I didn't know if I was in the hospital or out of it. Life was sketchy for me because the nerves in my body were shorted out. Reality came in pieces, like those of a jigsaw puzzle. I knew people and then I didn't know them. I knew where I was and then I was frightened because I was suddenly in a strange place. I was a shell of a person.

After being home a couple of days, for example, I found myself sitting at the kitchen table talking to a woman. She was sipping coffee and chattering away about people and events that I knew nothing about. I liked this woman. She had a familiar way about her and was very pleasant.

"Excuse me," I interrupted. "But who are you?"

There was shock on the woman's face. "Why Dannion, I'm your mother."

My stamina was also terribly depleted. I was able to stand for perhaps fifteen minutes at a time. Sometimes I could walk about ten steps, but after that I was so exhausted I had to sleep at least twenty hours.

When I was asleep, the real action took place. I returned to the Crystal City, where I attended classes taught by the Beings of Light.

These visions were not the same as those in the near-death experience. This time I was aware of my physical body and also of a different way of teaching by the Beings. When I was in a spirit form, I was bathed in knowledge and had only to think about something to understand it. These classroom sessions were different in that I had to struggle to learn my lessons. The struggle came in the way the class was taught. I was shown the equipment I was supposed to build, but I wasn't told much about it. Instead, I watched as the Spirit Beings operated the equipment. It was up to me to learn how to build it by deduction. I was shown the seven components of the bed, for example but was not told their names. And I saw how the eight parts of the centers worked, but I was not given a technical manual showing how to put them together.

This method of learning by watching and deduction made my mission an extremely difficult one. It also left me with some puzzles that I have yet to solve.

At one point, for instance, I was given a tour of the operating room of the future. There were no scalpels or sharp instruments in this operating room. Instead, all healing was done by special lights. Patients were given medications and exposed to these lights, said a Being who was with me, and that changed the vibration of cells within the body. Every part of the body has its own vibratory rate, said the Being. When that rate changes, certain illnesses take place. These lights return a diseased organ to its proper vibratory rate, healing whatever illness was plaguing it.

These medical visions were given to me as visions of a distant future. They didn't relate to my mission of building the centers other than to show the effects of stress on the human organism.

I was lucky to have such a rich spiritual life because my physical life was a shambles. Two months after the accident, I was sleeping far less but still had to struggle to do ordinary things. Just to get out of bed and into the living room required the planning of a major trip. For awhile, I tried to walk down the hall, but I kept blacking out and waking up with my face pressed against the floor. One morning I got out of bed and fell against the floor. I must have hit hard because, when I woke up, a puddle of blood was streaming from my broken nose. The accident dazed me so much that I lay there the entire day, until Sandy came home.

On a typical morning I would wake up well past eight o'clock, after Sandy had left for work. It took me as long as an hour and a half to get out of bed, since the long hours of sleep had left my muscles sore and tight.

After getting down on all fours, I would crawl on my belly to the living room and spend my day sitting on the couch, too exhausted to move. I often went in my pants because I was too tired and slow to make it to the toilet in time. When I ate the food that Sandy left for me on the coffee table, I always used a spoon. When I used a fork, I simply couldn't find my mouth, and I invariably stuck myself in the eye or forehead with it. The first time this happened I was trying to eat a piece of chicken and poked myself so hard in the forehead that I drew blood. I couldn't eat anything tricky like peas, because I was so shaky that they rolled off the spoon and onto the floor.

Most days I sat in the living room and did nothing. I didn't listen to music or watch television and I was so ashamed at being unable to remember my friends' names that I didn't ask them to come over and visit.

Most of the time I didn't mind being alone. The more time I spent alone, the more time I had to think about the visions. Alone in the living room or on the front porch, I would churn over the material from the nightly sessions with my spirit teachers. I would continuously do mathematical calculations in my mind and process the information that came into it. At times I joked that I was going to get smart enough to build the starship *Enterprise*.

It was good that I had a constant stream of visions, because I had nothing else to entertain me. I rarely went anywhere because the effort was so great. And if I did, I ran the risk of having blackout spells. Sometimes these could be quite embarrassing.

On New Year's Eve, for example, Sandy and I went to a Chinese restaurant to celebrate. I was determined to make it into the restaurant under my own power, and I wouldn't let her roll me in a wheelchair. From a parking spot for the handicapped I made my way slowly across the parking lot using two walking sticks. I called this "crabbing," because I looked like a half-dead crab with big pincers dragging itself across dry land.

It took between ten and twenty minutes to get into the restaurant, and by then I was breathing heavily from exhaustion. We were seated immediately, but I still couldn't catch my breath. Sandy ordered wonton soup while I sat there panting like a dog. I tried to carry on a conversation with Sandy, even though I could see the fear in her eyes over the distress that I was experiencing.

The waiter delivered two piping-hot bowls of the soup to our table. I looked down at the soup and then suddenly I was in it. I had blacked out and fallen face first into the bowl. At first Sandy thought it was a joke, but when I began to sputter and cough, she screamed and pulled my head up. Soup ran out of my nose and across the tablecloth. The waiter held me upright in the chair until I regained consciousness, and then the restaurant staff helped me get back into the car.

Even going outside on my own had its risks. One day I decided to spend the morning sitting in the sun. I "crabbed" my way through the house and out to the backyard. Slowly I stumbled to a chair in the middle of the yard. I was exhausted and drenched in sweat by the time I got to it. I groped for the armrests and like an old man began easing myself into it. The next thing I knew I was flat on my face in the grass. I had blacked out again and was unable to get up.

I lay there for six hours, until Sandy came home to pick me up. In that period of time I tried to find pleasure in examining the grass and dirt.

Perhaps the worst of these blackouts came when I went out to the car to get a magazine that I had left on the front seat. I grabbed the door, pulled it open and collapsed. When I awoke, my hand was stuck in the door handle and I was hanging by my hand with my shoulder out of socket. I had to dangle there for three hours until someone came to help.

By the end of 1975 I was broke. My hospital bills and loss of income exceeded $100,000, and the debt was climbing with each passing day. To pay my bills I was forced to sell everything I owned. All of my cars went first—five peak-condition antique automobiles sold to the highest bidder. Since I couldn't work, I had to sell my interest in my business, too. The nature of the independent contracting that I did for the government changed. I had worked in security, a job that required me to be inconspicuous and fast. There was no opening for a half-blind person who walked like a crippled crab. Now I was limited to office work. Leaving the fieldwork didn't bother me too much. Although it was much more exciting than life in the office, it carried with it many bad memories. As I saw in my near-death experience, I had done many things to hurt people through the years. After reliving those events, I didn't want any more of them to mar my record. As I told anyone who would listen, "Be careful what you do in life, because you have to see yourself do it again when you die. The difference is that this time you are on the receiving end."

We moved to another house because living in the old one served as a constant reminder of the lightning strike. So potent were the memories that I never went back into the bedroom where the strike occurred. I insisted that Sandy keep that door shut, and I refused to go anywhere near it, even though it was the largest bedroom in the house.

Before selling the house, I had the carpet changed in the bedroom. I had to have this done since an imprint of my feet was burned into it, which would have lowered the value of the house in much the way that the white outline of a homicide victim would. When the workmen pulled the carpet up, I was sitting on the living room sofa. I heard one of them whistle and the other one say, "Look at that!" Then one of them came out with a grin on his face and said, "There's black lines all across the floor where the electricity snaked out and found the nails!"

I had only a passing interest in the fact that I was broke. We received help from my parents and Sandy had a job, but I had lost everything I ever had to that bolt of lightning. By the time I became productive again, I had spent tens of thousands of dollars on medical bills. I haven't paid them off yet.

All I could think about were the centers that the Being had revealed to me. The centers were my destiny, they were what

I was supposed to do. I had to build these centers, but I didn't know how I was going to do it.

I talked constantly about "the centers," to myself and to anyone who would listen—and even those who wouldn't. They were the meaning of my life, and I had to get them built. I began to talk in detail about what had happened when I died, or at least I *tried* to talk in detail. Much of what I said in those days was hard for people to understand. It was clear in my head, but when it came out of my mouth, there were large pieces missing that made it sound as though I were speaking nonsense.

Nonetheless, I continued to talk about the whole experience, from leaving my body and visiting this heavenly place to seeing the future in boxes and finding out that I was destined to build these centers. I described all of this in detail because it was so firmly planted in my brain that there was no other way to explain it.

I explained the centers' eight steps more times than I can remember. I told people about the boxes and the visions of the future that they held. "These centers can change the future," I said. "They can reduce stress and fear, which cause many of the world's problems."

The more I talked, the more I felt people pulling away from me. Even Sandy was becoming more distant, and frankly, I couldn't blame her. She was a beautiful young woman with a long life ahead of her. Why should she squander it on a man who walked like a crab and babbled about heavenly stress-reduction projects?

And my friends, guys I had played football and drunk beer with for years, were now listening to me talk like a messiah. One of them hit it on the head when he said I sounded like a "retarded fundamentalist." That is exactly what I sounded like. They had never heard of a near-death experience, so they didn't have an inkling as to what had gone on.

In fact, *I* had never heard of a near-death experience. But I knew there was a great and powerful and glorious God, and I knew that the world on the other side was magnificent. In this world, I was living, breathing, and feeling the pain of the world.

I also knew that through love and God, I could work my way out of this pain. No one could tell me that the centers wouldn't work, even if they were just a vision at that point. I knew they could, because I had been every one of the people who could be helped by them. There was nothing anyone could tell me about pain. There was nothing anyone could tell me about mental anguish. I knew about pain and horror as no one knows it.

And I knew that the centers were the answer to helping mankind.

One day someone asked me why I didn't commit suicide. I can't remember who it was, but I do remember telling them the whole story as I have recounted it up to now, and their saying, "Dannion, if it was so great up there, why don't you kill yourself?"

I wasn't angered by the question at all. In fact, it was a very logical one, especially given the fact that I spent my waking hours singing the praises of the afterlife. Why didn't I kill myself?

Until that point I hadn't really thought about it. Sitting there on the porch like a zombie, I began to realize the change that had taken place in me as a result of the near-death experience. Regardless of my condition, the experience gave me the inner strength to endure. In my worst moments, all I had to do was recall the love that I felt emanating from those heavenly lights and I could press on. I knew that it would be wrong to take my own life, but the fact is, I never even thought of doing so. When things got bad, all I had to do was think of the love in that light and they got better.

When I say things got better, I mean that they got better somewhere deep inside of me, in a place that would let me live with this adversity. To the outside world, I was a different story. I could barely walk and had difficulty seeing. I had to wear welding goggles in the daytime and I weighed 155 pounds, about 70 pounds under my normal weight. My body was bent so that I looked like a question mark. I ranted and raved like a religious madman, talking about spiritual beings, a city of light, boxes with visions of the future, and, of course, the centers.

I sounded mad and probably should have been committed to a mental hospital. I might have been, too, had I not seen an article in the newspaper that changed my life again.

8

A Saving Grace

The article was no longer than four paragraphs, but reading those words changed my life every bit as much as the lightning bolt. They said simply:

Dr. Raymond Moody will be speaking at the University of South Carolina on "What Happens to Some People Who Have Been Declared Clinically Dead but Survive."

Moody, a Georgia psychiatrist, has been analyzing case studies of people who have almost died, only to return from their brush with death to talk about seeing dead relatives, Beings of Light and having their life pass before them in review.

Moody calls this phenomenon "the near-death experience," and says it may happen to thousands of people who have brushes with death.

I was excited. For the first time since being struck by lightning, I realized that I was not alone. After reading these few paragraphs, I understood that other people had been up that tunnel and seen the Beings of Light, too. I even had a name for what had happened—a near-death experience.

I looked at the date of the talk and realized it was only two days away. I had left the house only a few times since coming home, and those had been embarrassing incidents, but I decided I had to see Dr. Moody's presentation. If nothing else, I had to talk to someone who truly understood what I was going through.

Even though 1975 is not that long ago, it was the Dark Ages for people who had had near-death experiences. Doctors knew little or nothing about them and would usually dismiss them as bad dreams or hallucinations if they were mentioned by patients. If a patient persisted in talking about his experience, he was generally referred to a psychiatrist. Instead of listening and trying to understand, many psychiatrists medicated patients who had experienced these spiritual events. Clergymen were of surprisingly little help, usually considering these spiritual journeys to be the work of the devil.

There are many stories that illustrate the poor handling of

these experiences, but one of the most interesting to me was that of a soldier in the Korean War who nearly died in combat. He had a concussion, resulting from an enemy artillery barrage, and was taken to the hospital with very serious head injuries. Shortly after the explosion occurred, he left his body and drifted above the battlefield. He saw himself surrounded by other dead and wounded soldiers and began to feel sorry for his friends as well as for the enemy. Then he felt himself accelerating into a dark place and heading for a bright light. When he reached the light he got "soaked in good feelings." He had a review of his life that still leaves him stupefied for its vivid detail. "It was like a movie that was being watched by every sense in my body," he said. At the end of his review he was given a special message. "Just love everybody," a voice said in his head. Then he came back to life.

Within a couple of days he began talking about his experience, first to doctors and nurses, and then to other patients. The problem was, he talked too much. The doctors, who knew nothing about near-death experiences, referred him to military psychiatrists, who had no knowledge of them either. Before long, this very fine soldier with the spiritual message "just love everybody" found himself in a mental hospital.

The doctors' ignorance was understandable. Although such experiences have been reported in great numbers throughout the history of mankind, these reports have been published in history books or religious documents, not in medical textbooks.

Several episodes in the Bible, for instance, could only be near-death experiences. Paul the disciple had one after being stoned nearly to death at the gates of Damascus. High religious leaders such as popes have long collected tales of church members who have had brushes with a spirit world through near death. Pope Gregory the Fourteenth was so fascinated by these accounts that he met with the people who'd had near-death experiences.

The Mormon Church has collected many such experiences in the *Journal of Discourse,* a commentary on Mormon beliefs written by the church elders. Their findings match everything that happened to me. They believe that upon the death of the physical body, the spirit retains the five senses of sight, feeling, taste, hearing, and smell. They feel that death leaves us free of illness and disability and that the spirit body can move with great speed, see in many different directions at the same time, and communicate in ways other than speech.

My guess is that these beliefs were derived from personal experiences. Many of the Mormon elders have had near-death experiences or gathered detailed accounts of them from fellow churchgoers. They have drawn many conclusions about life after death from these experiences.

Death, for instance, is defined as "merely a change from one status or sphere of existence to another." About knowledge, the book says, "There, as here, all things will be natural, and you will understand them as you now understand natural things." They even deal with the heavenly light that I saw, in saying, "The brightness and glory of the next apartment is inexpressible."

They describe the near-death experience without using the actual term. "Some spirits who have experienced death are called back to inhabit their physical bodies again," reads the

Journal. "These persons pass through the natural or temporal death twice."

One such experience happened to Jedediah Grant as he lay on his deathbed and was told to his friend Heber Kimball, who recorded it for the *Journal:*

> He said to me, Brother Heber, I have been into the spirit world two nights in succession, and of all the dreads that ever came across me, the worst was to have to return to my body, though I had to do it.
>
> He saw his wife, she was the first person that came to him. He saw many that he knew, but did not have conversations with any but his wife Caroline. She came to him and he said that she looked beautiful and had their little child, that died on the plains, in her arms, and said, "Mr. Grant, here is little Margaret: you know that the wolves ate her up; but it did not hurt her, here she is all right."

Even though near-death experiences have been reported for thousands of years, they didn't enter the medical realm in full force until the 1960s, when advances in medical technology enabled many nearly dead patients to be brought back to life. Suddenly, people who had suffered heart attacks or had been severely injured in car accidents could be saved by a high-tech combination of machines, drugs, and skill.

People who would previously have died were surviving. And when they came back to full consciousness, they told stories that were very similar to those recorded through history and even those being told in other parts of the hospital by other patients who had been near death. The problem was that most doctors ignored these experiences, referring the patients to clergymen or telling them that such things couldn't have taken place. These wizards of technical medicine were equipped to handle almost any physical problem that arose, but spiritual problems were out of their realm.

Dr. Moody decided to listen to these stories and analyze them as no one else had. His first exposure to a near-death experience came in 1965, when he was studying philosophy at the University of Virginia. There he listened to Dr. George Ritchie, a local psychiatrist, tell about an extraordinary near-death experience he had had when he almost died of pneumonia in the army. The young soldier left his body after doctors declared him dead and found that he was able to travel across the country, his spirit zooming like a low-flying jet airplane. When he returned to the military hospital in Texas where he had died, he roamed the hospital in search of his body. He was finally able to locate it, not because he recognized his own face, but because he remembered the class ring that he wore on his finger.

Ritchie's experience was so intriguing to Moody that he never forgot it. In 1969 he began to talk about it in a philosophy class he was teaching. After one class session, a student came forward and told him about an experience he had had at the point of death. Moody was amazed at its similarity to Dr. Ritchie's. Over the next three years, he heard approximately eight more cases.

Moody went on to medical school but continued to collect these real-life stories from people who knew he was interested in their "afterlife" experiences. Eventually, he heard more than 150 stories.

Moody published most of these accounts in *Life After Life,* a book that introduced the field of medicine known as *near-death studies.* This book remains a great contribution to human understanding and has sold millions of copies worldwide. No longer could the informed physician tell a patient that the spirit world he had seen before being resuscitated was just a dream. Moody's research proved that it was a common experience, one that was had by many, if not most, people who survived a brush with death.

He called these episodes "near-death experiences." He further defined them by looking at all the case studies he had collected and finding the common elements. He found fifteen such elements, but no single person who reported all of the elements, although a few reported as many as twelve. Since *Life After Life* was published, these elements have been combined and reduced to nine common traits:

A sense of being dead,   in which a person knows he is dead.

Feelings of peace and painlessness,   in which a person who should be in considerable pain finds that he no longer feels his body.

An out-of-body experience,   in which a person's spirit or essence floats above his body and he is able to describe events that he shouldn't have been able to see. My hovering above Sandy, watching her pound on my chest, and my returning to my dead body in the hospital are two examples from my own NDE.

A tunnel experience,   in which the "dead" person has the sensation that he is traveling rapidly up a tunnel. This is what happened to me in the ambulance when, after I saw that I was dead, I ventured up a tunnel to the spiritual world.

Seeing people of light. Dead relatives who seem to be composed of light are often seen at the end of the tunnel. In my case, I saw many other people like myself who were composed of light, but none of them were departed relatives.

Being greeted by a particular being of light. In my case, the spirit guide I met at the end of the tunnel fits this description. He guided me in and out of the spirit world and caused me to have a life review. Other people describe going to a place, like a garden or forest, and meeting the Being of Light.

Having a life review, in which the person is able to see his entire life and evaluate all of its pleasant and unpleasant aspects. For me, this came through contact with my spirit guide.

Feeling a reluctance to return. I, too, did not want to return. But I was forced to by the Beings of Light and given the mission of building the centers.

Having a personality transformation, something positive for most people in that they cease to take things like nature and their families for granted. I experienced this kind of transformation, but I also had what most consider to be a negative transformation, too. I obsessed on my experience and my new mission on earth, which was to build "the centers." This obsession led to frustration, since I didn't know how I was supposed to build them.

When he was working on *Life After Life,* Moody had never met anyone who had experienced all of the traits of a near-death experience. I may have been the first one.

I went to the university where Moody was speaking dressed in my usual attire. I must have been a sight to behold. Since I knew the lighting at some of these events could be quite bright, I showed up wearing my welder's goggles. Around my shoulders I wore a long marine trenchcoat that hit me about midcalf. I carried two walking canes out in front of me and went clicking down the hall of the university building, looking for the right room.

"That guy looks like a praying mantis!" someone shouted when I walked into the lecture hall. There were about sixty people in the room, and I found a seat at the back to avoid a conspicuous walk to the front. There I sat and listened to Moody talk about my soul brothers and sisters.

He was just writing *Life After Life* at the time, and the marvel in his voice at his own research captivated everyone in the room. It was especially enthralling to me, since I had been there. *I was not alone! Others had been there too!*

I was energized by Dr. Moody's talk. I had been cracking from the strain, ready to give up. I had lost everything, I didn't know which way to go or what to do, and all of a sudden here was a savior, someone who understood what I was going through. All of a sudden I felt new strength.

At the end of his talk, Moody stepped forward and asked, "Is there anyone in this room who has had one of these experiences?"

My hand went up.

"I had something like that," I said in my halting speech. "I was struck by lightning."

I was surprised to find that Moody had read a newspaper article about me and remembered the incident. He collected potential case studies, and one way he did this was to clip stories from newspapers about people who'd had near-fatal accidents. He had been planning to contact me for some time.

"Can I come to interview you?" he asked.

Of course, I said. "At least I'd have someone to talk to who wouldn't run away."

The room filled with laughter. Everyone found this funny except Dr. Moody and me. He seemed to know exactly how I felt. If anyone could have seen beneath the welder's goggles, they would have seen that I was ready to cry. Instead, I began to laugh. I tried to keep from shaking, but the laughter came so strong that I soon found myself almost hooting.

"What's so funny?" someone next to me asked.

"If someone had told me about a near-death experience before I had my own, I would have made fun of them," I said. "Now I am one."

9

A New Lease on Life

D r. Raymond Moody has been described by close friends as being a cross between Donald Duck and Sigmund Freud. He is at once brilliant and comical, a man who can weave one-liners in with the works of Plato. So smart was Raymond as a student that he taught at the Medical College of Georgia while he was a student there.

I recognized Raymond's intellect and his humor immediately when he came to my house about a week later. He pulled into the driveway in an ancient blue Pontiac with crayon drawings all over the doors. They were stick figures that his young sons had created, and they looked like the kind of drawings that can be seen in the caves of prehistoric man.

"He's driving Fred Flintstone's car," I thought as I peeked through the curtain.

He walked up the stairs and banged on the screen door. I had already gotten up, but it took me a couple of minutes to struggle to the front door. Raymond waited patiently while I shuffled across the room and pushed the door open.

When he saw the living room, it was love at first sight. I had seven rocking chairs, and I soon discovered that Raymond always sits in a rocking chair when he does his serious thinking.

He sat down in a straight-backed oak chair with big rockers on it, and I scraped across the floor and sat facing him in an upholstered swivel rocker. There we literally rocked around the clock, talking for eight hours about what had happened to me and about near-death experiences in general. *Life After Life* was not yet published, but already Raymond had a number of new ideas and was working on another book.

Before he told me anything about either book, he interviewed me about my experience. That way, he explained, no one could ever claim that what I had to say was jaded by the findings he was going to publish.

He interviewed me in a very flat way, asking open-ended questions and responding in a deadpan fashion. He showed no emotion as I told him of my experience and the developments that sprang from it. He just asked to hear more until there was nothing more to hear.

The goal of this method of interviewing is to keep the subject from embellishing his story. By asking brief, open-ended questions and not relating others' near-death experiences, Raymond could be certain that he was not coloring my experience with those of others.

Although the flat approach Raymond used is the best way to elicit the truth, I found it disconcerting. I was accustomed to having people gape in awe as I recounted what happened. But Raymond just sat straight-faced and listened as I talked. He showed no alarm or surprise when I told him about the cathedrals of light. "Yes, yes, I've heard of those before," he said. Even hearing about the halls of knowledge didn't cause him to lift an eyebrow.

I told him about the beauty and the glory of the spirit world, and how all the light in this place was knowledge. I told about the belief of these heavenly spirits that we are "powerful spiritual beings" who are exhibiting great courage in coming to earth.

I even remember some of the exact words that I said to him: "I knew everything in the world and the universe. I knew the destiny of everything in the world. Even the simplest things, like a raindrop. Do you know that there isn't a raindrop anywhere whose destiny is anything but to make it back to the sea? That's what we are trying to do, Raymond. We are just raindrops trying to get back to the source, the place from where we came.

"Those who come here are courageous, because we are willing to experiment in a world that is so confining when compared to the entire universe. The spirits say that everyone who is here should hold himself in high esteem."

I told him about the boxes of knowledge, but I didn't tell

him what information they contained. I was moving so fast through the narrative at this point that I skipped over the details.

Then I told him about the centers, in particular about the bed. I was obsessing about the bed all the time now, wondering where I would get the parts for it, wondering even *what* the parts were, since I could see them but couldn't actually identify them.

I told Raymond everything and told it with such fury that it must have seemed a frightening tirade, like the ravings of a demented man. I know that is how my story came across to everyone else, since they said outright that I sounded as if I were crazy or just avoided me as if I were. That didn't happen with Raymond. He stopped rocking and leaned forward, looking deep into my eyes.

"You aren't crazy," he said. "I have never heard a story as detailed as yours, but I have heard other stories with the elements of yours. You are not crazy. You have just experienced something that has made you unique. It's like discovering a new country with different people and trying to convince everyone that such a place exists."

A hard spot inside me melted as what he said filled me with comfort. I realized I would now find others just like me who had seen this "new country." I felt a burst of fresh energy. I knew I was going to come back and that nothing was going to stop me.

For the rest of the day, Raymond told of some of the case studies he had uncovered during his research. Studying these experiences and writing about them had caused Raymond's life to change dramatically. His first book wasn't even out yet, but a newspaper article about his work had been published in the *Atlanta Constitution,* and already he was swamped with phone calls from people who'd had NDEs. This was a new experience for Raymond, who up until then had led a quiet, almost academic, life. "When this book comes out I won't have any time for myself," said Raymond. He was concerned about this loss of privacy, especially about what it would do to his study time. If there are two things Raymond likes to do, I found out later, it is read and think.

After Raymond left that day, there was a definite change in my attitude. I began to fight back. I tried to stop feeling so sorry for myself. This was no small task, since I was so badly physically damaged that I never dreamed I would be normal again. But instead of acting as if I had been dealt an insurmountable blow, I began to look at the positive side of my life, at the ways in which I was overcoming my injuries. For instance, it now took me about twenty minutes to make it down the hall and to the bathroom, where only weeks before I was usually unable to make it in time to keep from soiling myself. The light still hurt my eyes, but less so with each new day. Movement and strength were returning to my hands, and the general pain caused by the lightning burns was slowly going away.

Psychologically I was improving even faster. My level of ranting and raving dropped a notch or two. I still talked constantly about my experience with anyone who would listen, but I no longer sounded like an insane fundamentalist preacher. Because of Raymond's understanding and the knowledge that there were many others like me, I no longer had to convince anyone that this experience had taken place. I began to read the Bible, studying the nature of the visions that take place in the scriptures. I also read *Life After Life,* which Raymond gave me in manuscript form.

Raymond and I talked almost daily now. During one of our phone calls, he remembered that I had not told him the future as revealed to me in the boxes. Would I mind telling him? he asked. We made an appointment to get together.

A couple of nights later, Sandy and I showed up at Raymond's house. We were invited into the living room, where Raymond offered us each a soda. Then we began to talk about the thirteen boxes and what they revealed. I told him of a great war that would take place in the deserts of the Middle East in the nineties that would destroy a major army and change the complexion of that part of the world. I told him how the Soviet Union would collapse and how there would be food riots and political turmoil as the Soviets tried to find a new political system to replace communism. I then told him how the world would become increasingly balkanized, with big countries breaking up into little ones. I described the contents of each box that the spirit beings showed me, just as I have in this book.

Our discussions took place over several nights. Raymond sat and rocked, sometimes jotting down notes. He also wrote down much of what I said, nodding as he listened. Among Raymond's many attributes is that he is a great listener. He knows that people love to talk and that the best way to know the truth about someone is to soak up everything he is willing to tell you. So he listened and I talked.

Then I shocked him. I told him that we would be together on the day when the world began to collapse. We would know then, I said, that all of the visions I had seen in the boxes would come true.

"Where will we be?" Raymond asked.

"We will be in the Soviet Union when it falls apart," I said. "We will be there and we will know ourselves that all of this stuff is true."

"I see," he said, writing something down in his notebook. I could tell that he didn't believe what I was saying, and I had a hard time believing it myself. The Soviet Union was a closed country in the seventies, and travel visas for American citizens were extremely difficult to arrange. What is more, my employment in sensitive areas of the U.S. government made it unlikely that I would ever get a chance to travel to this country under any circumstances other than an official visit. And Raymond and his book were banned by the Soviets and considered subversive.

Still, the vision from the box had me in the streets of Moscow with a man I couldn't identify, watching people lined up and waiting for food. As I sat with Raymond that night, I had a deep sense that the man I would be with during this momentous occasion was Raymond.

This scene came true. I have to tell you now that Raymond and I visited Moscow in 1992, just after the collapse of communism, and watched downtrodden Russians line up around the block in scant hope of entering stores and buying whatever food was available. When this happened, Raymond looked at me with surprise as he remembered that night almost fifteen years earlier. "This is it!" he said. "This is the vision you saw in the box!"

. . .

T hose early days of visiting Raymond are some of the best I have ever had. Sandy and I would have dinner with Raymond, his wife, and their two boys. Although he was beset by telephone calls from others who wanted to talk about their experiences, Raymond took a special liking to me.

Because of the subject matter he was dealing with, Raymond had become the only hope for understanding for many people. Remember, almost no one talked about these experiences in those days, and when they did, they were treated like nut cases. People sought Raymond out because he was a medical doctor who understood.

On the telephone, people had a pleading in their voices that would bring pain to Raymond's face. As they told him how they almost died, it was not uncommon for Raymond to put his hand to his mouth and say, "Oh no!" while visibly expressing shock at what he had just heard. He really cared deeply about these people and would talk to them like family members.

He would leave the dinner table to take one of these phone calls, and he never asked the caller if he could call back later.

I only heard Raymond's side of these conversations, laced with comments like "Yes, many people I have spoken to have seen dead relatives at the end of this tunnel," or, "Leaving your body is common during near-death experiences."

Hearing Raymond talk to other people about near-death experiences was soothing for me. I could tell that these people were as perplexed by their experiences as I was about mine. I felt myself relaxing more and more.

As I felt more at ease with Raymond, I told him more and more about the predictions of the future that I had witnessed. As I have already said, I discussed these in great detail, from Chernobyl to the wars. I don't think he believed any of the visions would come true, but at least he jotted them down, which was a big help later when the visions became realities.

10

My Own Kind

From the moment *Life After Life* was published in late 1975, Raymond's life became a whirlwind. He was in Charlottesville, working on his residency in psychiatry, when a deluge of requests started coming in from all quarters. The media wanted interviews, organizations and universities wanted him to lecture, and as always, people just wanted to talk. The demands of completing his residency kept Raymond from dealing firsthand with many of these requests.

One day Raymond's first wife, Louise, called me and asked if I would give him a hand. He needed some help in scheduling talks and interviews, an organizational skill that he had neither time nor patience for. By now it was the end of 1976, and I had improved greatly. My doctors no longer told me I was going to die soon, although they did say that the heart damage I had suffered was a detriment to my "long-term survival." The welding goggles were gone, replaced by a pair of very dark sunglasses that I wore only when outside. I could now walk with only one cane, at least most of the time, and I was able to speak coherently and not go off into a hapless babble about the "cities of light" and my visions of the future.

I don't want you to think that I had forgotten about any of it. No, my near-death experience was always right there, about two inches in front of my face. I was just able to control myself and bring it up at appropriate times. Raymond helped me do that, too, by telling me to "quit thinking you're Jesus Christ and wait until people ask before you start preaching to them about what happened."

I went up to Charlottesville to give Raymond a hand. At times Raymond would not come out of his library, and this was one of them. He was hard at work on his second book, *Reflections on Life After Life,* and clearly did not want to be disturbed.

That left plenty for me to do. I answered the telephone, fielded requests for media interviews, and set up a speaking schedule that had Raymond traveling to the far corners of the world. I went to many of these speaking engagements, too. I wanted to be there to handle the business, but these were also opportunities for me to be surrounded by hundreds of my own kind, people who'd had near-death experiences and were now discovering others like themselves for the first time.

This is a luxury afforded to surprisingly few near-death

experiencers. Even today, when the experience is well recognized, it is rare for the "experienced" to get together. Back then, the results of these meetings were remarkable.

For instance, at a speaking engagement in Washington, D.C., a woman came forward after Raymond's talk and told me about her experience:

When I was a young woman, we went to California on vacation. Before we left, I had been having extreme pain in my right side that just got worse and worse as the vacation went on. Finally, my husband took me to the hospital.

The first doctor to look at me said that my appendix was ready to rupture. The second doctor to examine me said that my pain was caused by infection. The third doctor said that it was a tubal pregnancy. The one thing they all agreed on was that I should have surgery immediately.

When they opened me up, they found that the first diagnosis was right. My appendix had burst, and I now had a massive infection in my stomach area about the size of a small melon.

I spent over a month in the hospital, much of it in a coma. On one of these days, my family was told that I was going to die. They gathered around me, and it looked as though the doctors were right. I had pneumonia, my veins collapsed, and my breathing was failing.

I could hear everything that was going on in the room. I could hear my family crying and praying, and I could hear the nurses talking and the doctors coming and going. It was like I was fully conscious; I just couldn't respond.

Then suddenly I took off! It was like being on a roller coaster. I zoomed and boy was it fun! When we stopped, I was in a place that was as real as the city I am in now. I knew where I was—I was in heaven!

I walked through a meadow of waving green grass until I came to an angel. He was about seven feet tall. We walked together and were joined by other people I knew who had died. My great-uncle was there, and so was my big brother, both of whom had died in the last ten years or so. We were together as naturally as if we were right here on earth.

The angel and I went up a hill. He opened a beautiful gate and I went inside, where I stood inside a very bright yellow light. There were no labels in this place. They didn't ask me what church I belonged to, they just invited me to come right inside. I looked into a room that was absolutely brilliant with light, and I saw what I considered to be the Light of the Father. It was so bright that I had to look away.

As I looked away, I could see that the light reflected down a crystal boulevard that ran down the center of a city. I saw many other things, too, but one of the most interesting was that prayers were streaming through this heavenly world like rays of light. It was beautiful to see what becomes of our prayers.

This woman rallied and began to get well almost immediately. She came out of the coma and began talking about what she had seen. Her doctor was called back to the hospital from home. To his great embarrassment, he had signed a death certificate, and now he had to "unsign it," as she put it. When he arrived she became very excited and began telling him what she had seen. Surprisingly, he was unimpressed.

At the end of our conversation she began to cry. "You know," she told me, "I talked to my doctor about this and he said, 'Honey, that's something you need to talk to your minister about.' I talked to my minister and he said, 'Honey, you need to talk to your doctor about it.' "

When she said that, we both started laughing.

There were so many other stories. A man in Chicago told me this one:

I had what I think was an out-of-body experience when I was having bypass surgery. The doctors later told me that they had so much trouble starting my heart that they were ready to declare me dead.

What happened to me was a very living experience. I was transported to a big room that glowed like gold. I looked around the room and saw thousands of faces, like pictures all around me. My attention was drawn to one of these pictures. I went up and looked at it. It was the kindest face I have ever seen, and because I have always been a religious person, I like to think that maybe it was King David or perhaps King Solomon, but I really don't know who it was.

Anyway, as I looked at this picture, I heard a great

choir of thousands of voices. It was the most beautiful music I have ever heard. I turned and saw a chorus of thousands of people really singing it up.

That experience was confirmation of a heavenly afterlife for this man, though others interpreted it differently. "A few days later I told my aunt what had happened and she turned white like a sheet," the man told me. "She said, 'Keep it to yourself. Stuff like that can only happen to people who are in touch with the devil.' "

A man in Atlanta had been in a motorcycle accident that left him with a lacerated liver. Blood poured from his liver into his body cavity, and he began blacking out. It was some time before the attending physician stopped checking his head for a concussion and discovered that he was bleeding internally. By the time he got to surgery, he had lost enough blood to be dead.

While the doctors began cutting, this man found himself drifting upward into a heavenly light. He could turn over and see his body being worked on by doctors below. He remembers thinking that he should have been afraid but he wasn't.

"A voice kept telling me to take it easy, that everything would be okay," he said. "Then I just sort of rolled over and settled back down into my body. I talked to my doctor about it and he never even looked up from the clipboard that he was writing on. "He just grinned like he knew everything and said, 'It was probably just a dream.' "

Scientists now agree that near-death experiences are *not*

dreams. Dreams happen to people who are asleep and are associated with specific brain waves. But this doctor's proclamation was disturbing to the man, who knew very well the difference between dreams and reality. What he experienced was real, and it wasn't until now, surrounded by others like himself, that he had the reality of this experience confirmed for him.

Nurses came forward too. I have found that although doctors tend to ignore these experiences, nurses listen to them and use them to help patients heal.

For example, a nurse in California told me about a patient dying of cancer who had a predeath vision. She saw her aunt, who had been dead for more than ten years, standing at the end of her bed. The woman was glowing with a heavenly light and looked pain-free and happy. "We'll be with each other soon," she said. A few seconds later, she disappeared.

When the oncologist made his rounds in the morning, the woman told him what she had seen. She was excited at the vision and its meaning. To her it clearly meant that there was life after death. As the nurse put it, "This vision was the only good news this woman had had in six months."

The doctor listened to her with a deadpan expression. When she finished, he simply dismissed the story with a wave of his hand. "Sounds like a dream to me," he said.

The enthusiasm left this woman's face. When the doctor went out, she sank into the bed, her head almost disappearing into the pillow. The nurse immediately came to her rescue.

She propped another pillow under her head and said what a heartless fool she thought the doctor was.

"He doesn't notice things like that because he's interested in machines, not patients," she said. "Things like this happen to a lot of patients in your position, and I think they are something other than dreams."

The two went on to have a lengthy talk about visions and death. "Until that vision she had not been able to face the fact that she was dying," said the nurse. "But now she talked about it openly, and her own doctor missed that opportunity."

During these tours I met people who had spent years tormented by the fact that they had had a powerful spiritual experience that no one would discuss with them. I heard horror stories from people who were made fun of by family members because they had seen the same heavenly places that I had seen. These were healing experiences for me as well as the people I met because finally we were together, and finally we understood.

I found many of the stories these people told so fascinating that I began writing them down, amassing case studies of my own. Here are several that I collected:

"THE GATES WERE MADE OF GIGANTIC PEARLS"

In Chicago a woman approached me, walking with the sort of stiffness that indicated a back injury. She introduced herself and then wasted no time in telling me why she had come to the talk:

In a very short period of time, my sister was killed in a car wreck, my best friend died, and I broke my back. I was rear-ended at a very high rate of speed by another automobile. It was a wonder that I wasn't paralyzed by the accident, and even more of a wonder that I didn't die during surgery.

I was in surgery for four hours to fuse two vertebrae. The doctors readily admitted that they gave me too much anesthetic and that my heart stopped a number of times in the operating room and even in recovery.

At some point in all of this, I went through a dark place and found myself in the presence of the Lord. I was right there!

You might find it hard to believe, but I stood before gates that led right into heaven! The gates were made of gigantic pearls, twelve big ones that seemed to glow. The streets inside these gates were a golden color, and the walls of the buildings were so bright that I could barely see.

I saw a person of light that I think was Jesus. I couldn't see his face, but he was glowing gloriously and furiously. Even when I couldn't look at him, I could feel the glow, it was that strong.

I went to a garden that was filled with green grass and was lush with flowers and fruit trees. If someone picked an apple, for instance, the apple would grow right back.

I wandered through this garden, seeing other spirit beings like myself. Then I saw my sister! It was wonderful. We talked for a long time, and she told me how happy she was here in this place, which I guess was heaven.

We spent a long time together, talking and listening to the heavenly music that came from everything. It was so beautiful and peaceful, and naturally I wanted to stay.

After a while I had to go back and talk to the person I thought was Jesus. He told me that he loved me and wanted me to come back. I said that I wanted to stay right now, but he said that I had to go back to earth because he had something for me to do.

I wanted to know what it was that I had to do, but he wouldn't tell me directly. Instead he said, "You will know what it is every step of the way."

It was a relief for this woman to find others who had gone to this heavenly place. Her husband was tired of hearing about her experience, and her minister was making a sincere effort to distance himself from her. Whenever she came around, he got "real busy" with other things and had little or no time to devote to her.

"Since I told him what happened, he wants nothing to do with me," she said. "I no longer take it personally, though. I realize that most people just don't understand."

"I HAVE RECEIVED ANSWERS TO MY QUESTIONS"

An elderly woman I met in the Midwest felt misunderstood, too. She approached me and with great liveliness told about her "journey to heaven." She was so sharp and clever that I was shocked to find she was a victim of multiple strokes and had a bad heart. Here is her story:

I was in a hospital in Michigan where I had been taken because I was having strokes that were causing seizures. My heart wasn't strong enough to get me through these seizures, and it stopped. I felt the pain of cardiac arrest for a minute, and then a peaceful feeling came over me as I saw a light off to my right.

I was drawn to that light like a magnet to metal. As I got closer and closer, I felt love and understanding swelling inside me until I thought I was going to explode.

I came into this lighted area and there was a spirit made of incredible light that I think was Jesus.

I was hugged right into that light. It was a wonderful feeling, like being hugged by my dad, who loved me regardless of what I did. It was that kind of love.

And this light was more than light. It was made of millions and millions of tiny, diamondlike sparkles that glittered and had feeling. I knew I was a part of this light.

I went into a grassy area that was like a lovely pasture. I found my grandmother there, a woman who has been dead since I was a small child. I also found my uncle, who has been dead since my teenage years.

In a blink of an eye I left the grassy place and was back with Jesus. He said, "What have you done for your fellow man?" He asked it like a question, but there was also a sort of answer there, too, which was that I was going back to earth to actually do things for my fellow man.

People I have told this story to insist that I was having a dream, but this was totally different. I have had dreams and I have had drug reactions, and this was neither. It was real.

"I WANTED TO BE A PART OF THE LOVING LIGHT"

In the Deep South I met a lovely young woman who said she could understand completely what had happened to me, since the same thing had happened to her. During her pregnancy a few years earlier, she nearly died when a pain she was ignoring proved to be something serious:

> When I was about six months pregnant with my son, I started having pain underneath my right breast. I thought it was just heartburn, which pregnant women frequently have. But it got worse and worse, and it took longer and longer to ride out the pain.
>
> Finally, I woke up one night and the pain was so bad I could hardly keep from crying. I went into the bathroom and tried sitting in different positions, but nothing helped. The last thing I remember was sitting on the edge of the bathtub. Then I passed out and fell backwards.
>
> I felt like I was out of my body. I felt like I was going a thousand miles an hour, just surging up a tunnel. I passed several lights and headed for a very bright one that got brighter and brighter. Then I stopped.
>
> I didn't want to go into the light, but just standing there in front of it gave me a peaceful and joyful feeling

that was not easy to explain. The best I can do is to say that I wanted to stay and be a part of the light, and I didn't feel like I cared about anything else.

I didn't hear words, but a voice that came from somewhere said that I had to go back. I began to argue, but the voice reminded me in a very gentle way that there was someone inside of me and I owed it to him to go back. I still wanted to stay, but then another thing happened. The light made me feel the way my husband would feel if I died. I felt very sad then and wanted to return.

When I awoke, I was in the recovery room of our local hospital. My gall bladder had ruptured and I had nearly died. Luckily, I didn't, and my child was born in good health.

Few people understood near-death experiences back then, which usually left those of us who'd had them feeling like social outcasts. That wasn't the case with this woman. Her husband accepted her story as real, with the result that their relationship became stronger than it had ever been before.

"IT'S NOT HER TIME TO GO"

Near-death experiences are baffling for adults, so you can imagine the confusion that takes place in the mind of a child who lives to tell her parents about a journey into the light. A woman in Virginia told me of one such experience:

When I was eight years old, my appendix ruptured. I was taken to the hospital, where a frightened emergency-room doctor told my parents that I was going to die. I heard him say this, because he said it while standing over me.

They did surgery anyway. I was given ether and I blacked out. Then I was back. I was drifting above my body as the doctors cut away on my abdomen. "We're losing her! We're losing her!" one of them kept saying.

I was excited by this, because whatever was happening, I liked it. All of a sudden I was going through a dark tunnel and heading for a light at the other end. Then I found myself in a beautiful place with a big bright light that was beautiful and didn't hurt my eyes at all.

I looked around me and could see people that I didn't recognize. There was a silence, and then I heard a lady's voice in my head: "No, no, it is not her time to go. She has to go back."

"I don't want to go back," I thought.

"You have to," the voice said. "You have a good life ahead of you."

When I told my father about this later, his face turned pale and he got real nervous. "Don't tell anyone," he said. "This is our secret." So I didn't tell anyone, even though the experience has been with me every day since it happened. I thought maybe there was something wrong with me until I started hearing about the experiences that other people have had. Now I can finally talk openly about mine.

"WHAT YOU ARE DOING IS WRONG"

Many people told of how they had been transformed by their near-death experiences. But one of the most amazing of these stories came from a woman near Washington, D.C., who tried to kill herself. Here is her story:

> When I was a teenager, I decided to kill myself because my uncle was molesting me. I took a handful of pills and then went outside. I was very upset and fell to my knees and began to cry.
>
> I felt groggy and then fell over on my side. It was then that I heard a voice. It was evening, and I looked around to see who was talking. There, standing over me, was my grandmother. She had killed herself years ago because of chronic heart disease.
>
> She looked down at me and got right to the point. "What you are doing is wrong," she said. "You aren't supposed to kill yourself."
>
> The spot where my grandmother was standing was very dark, maybe because a spot next to her was becoming very bright, like a train coming through a tunnel. This light picked me up and held me close. "It's not your time," it said. "I have things for you to do."
>
> I staggered into the house and called the police, who saved me. I told only close friends about the experience, because who else could understand? I didn't think there was anyone else like me.

This woman's experience changed her life in many ways. Somehow, she said, it gave her a sense of the big picture. She realized that although she couldn't change what had already happened in her life, the future was a clean slate. Her grades improved and she began to volunteer in nursing homes. Now she is a registered nurse. "I chose a helping profession specifically because of my near-death experience," she told me.

"I WILL WALK YOU BACK"

Many people who almost die report seeing departed relatives. This didn't happen to me, largely, I think, because I hadn't lost anyone who was close to me. But a woman I met in Florida told me about her near-death experience, in which she saw a number of dead relatives, including a stillborn son:

> I almost died during childbirth. In all the straining that goes on, I burst a blood vessel and my blood pressure plummeted.
>
> I was in great pain and then suddenly I was out of my body, floating above my body. I watched the doctors for a while and then began floating higher and higher until I was above the ceiling and actually able to see the wiring.
>
> Then I went up a cave, and at the end I was with a number of people who looked just like me. I saw my grandparents, who had been dead for years, and an uncle who had been killed in the Korean War. Then a young man walked up to me, a child really. He said, "Hi, Mom," and I realized that this was the stillborn child I had had a few years earlier.
>
> I got to talk to him for quite some time and felt very happy that he was here in this place with his relatives. Then he took my hand and said, "You have to go back now. I will walk with you."
>
> I didn't want to go back, but he insisted. He walked with me and said goodbye. Then I was back in my body.

How could I tell this stuff to anyone? Who would believe it? My husband wouldn't even want to hear, it so I didn't tell him. But now I can talk, now that I know others have seen these things, too.

Although I met hundreds of people who'd had near-death experiences, I met very few who experienced all the things that I did. Most people went to what I call the first level, in which they go up the tunnel, see Beings of Light, and have a life review. Very few went to the city of light and the hall of knowledge.

One of those who did was a man who had grabbed hold of a thirteen-thousand-volt line without being grounded. The resulting surge of electricity blew both of his legs and one of his arms off. He came to one of Raymond's lectures and talked to me afterwards. The afterlife that he had experienced was the same as mine. He talked about rivers of energy that he crossed with a Being of Light. Although he had had no visions of the future as I did, he had visited a city of light that had the same glowing cathedrals and sense of omnipresent knowledge as the one I experienced.

I tried to talk with him in greater detail later, but he wouldn't say too much about what had happened. By nature he was a quieter, more private, person than I and had been made sullen by the skeptics who had heard his story and insisted that it couldn't have taken place.

Still, I persisted in trying to talk to him about his near-death experience, but I got nowhere. I couldn't break the ice with him as I usually could with others. He was also taking a substantial amount of pain medication, which made him even less communicative than he might have been.

I encountered other people during this time who had been to the city of lights. One was a Mormon man I met in Salt Lake City whose story was almost identical to mine. He saw the Beings of Light and the glorious cathedrals. Instead of referring to them as "spirits" or "Beings," however, he called them "angels," and he called the cathedrals "tabernacles."

In Chicago I met a woman who had been struck by lightning as a child. She was well dressed and appeared very sane and calm as she described going to the city of light and standing in the presence of what sounded like the same spiritual Beings I had talked to.

She said that the Beings trained her in a system of colors. Everything she did now was based on her intuitions about colors. When she bought a car, when she dressed in the morning, even when she decorated her office, she did so based on some color scheme that had been given her by the Beings of Light. I didn't understand exactly how this color system worked, but the result, she told me, was to bring her together with others like her who had been to the cathedrals of light.

"We're supposed to come together for something great," she said. "I don't know what it is, but I will know when we get together."

Suddenly I was meeting people who had not only had near-death experiences, but who'd had almost the *same* experience I had. Finding these people was a great relief. It was almost like coming to the surface after being held underwater by an unseen hand.

These meetings confirmed the reality of what had happened.

Perhaps one person like myself could have dreamed such a magnificent adventure. But could a number of people in different parts of the country have the same complex "dream" at the point of personal extinction? For me, the answer was clearly "no." We had really died and gone to a spiritual world. The only difference between what we had done and visiting a distant country was that we did it without taking our mortal bodies with us.

Meeting these people also convinced me that I was not insane. As you know by now, that was a concern of mine from the beginning, as it was for almost all the other near-death experiencers I was now meeting. We began to realize that we were special, not insane. This sense of being special came over us when we realized we were not alone. Instead of feeling ashamed or humiliated, we suddenly felt good about ourselves.

I should mention that Mormons did not make near-death experiencers feel crazy. Since the afterlife was a part of their church doctrine, they actually welcomed testimony on what had been seen and heard on the other side.

In 1977 I went to Spain, where I sat on a panel of people who had been clinically dead but survived. These people came from all over the world—from Europe, the United States, and Asia. As we told stories that were similar, I realized this was a universal experience.

Along with confidence in my sanity, I gained an even stronger feeling that I had been given a true mission: to build the centers. This mission was, in essence, my message. I never wanted to do any of this stuff, but only a fool would resist a mandate from God.

I never ran into anyone else who had been given such a

mission, nor did I ever meet anyone else who saw visions of the future—who sat before the thirteen Beings of Light and was presented the future a box at a time. When I got together with others, I was the only one to talk about such an event.

Still, I knew that it had happened. Parts of the vision were beginning to take place, and I could see subtle things happening in the world that seemed to indicate that the rest of the visions would also become reality. My confidence grew and I felt psychologically stronger.

"We are normal people," I remember saying in a panel discussion. "We are normal people who have had something paranormal happen to us."

Although I still looked a bit damaged from the lightning strike, I was indeed feeling more normal by the day.

Then I made a discovery that truly jolted me.

11
Special Powers

There was no "first time" that I realized I had psychic powers. I did realize something extraordinary was happening when a friend barked at me one day, "Dannion, why don't you keep your mouth shut and let me finish my questions before you answer them!"

The answer popped right out of my mouth. "Because I know what you are going to ask before you say it."

"No you don't!" the friend barked again.

"Okay, try this," I said, and I told him his next sentence. His jaw dropped, because it was exactly what he was about to say.

Then, as he began to speak, I talked along with him as though we had practiced it, saying the same thing he was saying at the same time he said it.

I began to experience this phenomenon with members of my family. It got to the point where I answered their questions before they were even asked. I didn't know how I was doing this. I just "heard" what they were going to say before they said it. This was as much a shock to me as it was to the baffled person to whom I was talking.

I remember doing this once at a seminar where I had been invited to speak about my experience. As people came up to talk to me, I would begin the conversation by asking the question that they were going to ask me before the words even left their mouths. This surprised some of them who then turned to others around them and said, "He read my mind."

My father was there too, and he couldn't believe what was happening. He had seen me do this before, but never in a setting made up entirely of strangers. As soon as I finished talking to someone, he would corner him and ask if I had truly read his mind. Nine out of ten people insisted that I had. By the time we left the seminar, my father was dazed and confused by what he had seen.

"How the hell do you do that?" he asked.

"I don't know," I shrugged. "I just don't know."

And I didn't. I didn't know that these questions hadn't been asked. I would hear the words in my head as surely as if the person had spoken them.

When I realized what was happening, I tried to tune into the other person. I found that if he hesitated when speaking, it was usually a sign that he was changing his train of thought. At that moment I could pick up his thought waves and hear what he was thinking.

My ability to read minds improved rapidly—so rapidly, in fact, that it almost ruined negotiations on a business deal. After this happened I realized that it was sometimes in my best interests to be quiet about the things I was "hearing."

My three partners and I were negotiating the sale of some electronic equipment with members of a Norwegian shipping company. We had worked on this deal for some time, and now three company officials from Norway had flown to South Carolina to hammer out the details of an agreement.

As we sat with the Norwegians at a conference table, they began to speak to one another in Norwegian. They were agreeing on the questions they were going to ask us before asking them in English. As they spoke in their native tongue, struggling with what they were going to say, I suddenly spoke up and said, "What you mean to ask us is . . ." and then I formulated the question for them. They laughed nervously, and we discussed the first portion of the contract that they had questions about.

Then they began to speak among themselves in Norwegian again, which I could understand perfectly by reading their minds. Once again I told them what they were thinking.

"We thought you did not speak our language," one of the Norwegians said.

"I don't," I said, and proceeded to tell them my story.

There was disbelief on the faces of everyone in the room. The Norwegians had trouble believing that a person could gain extrasensory powers as a result of being struck by lightning. My partners couldn't believe that I would talk about my experience in the middle of serious business negotiations. They were afraid that such a discussion might ruin the deal.

"No one wants their mind read," said one of my partners. "Especially when they are negotiating a contract."

I understood that completely and decided from that point on not to reveal what I knew during most business negotiations. But that didn't mean I didn't use my powers to keep people from taking advantage of me.

In one of my electronics businesses, we decided to buy a product from a new vendor. My partners and I liked this fellow, who made a component we needed for our masking system. We went to dinner with him and then out for drinks, and none of us suspected that anything was wrong, including me.

That all changed, however, when we sat down at the table to negotiate the deal. As we talked about pricing, a tone in his voice made me leery. As I listened to him, I picked up the image of a room filled with the product we were buying. As I scanned this room in my mind, I could tell that most of the components we were about to buy were defective. This man was trying to unload junk!

I told my partners what I had seen before we signed the contract. At our last round of negotiations we were able to insert a clause that allowed us a credit for every part that didn't work. In the end, more than sixty percent of the components had to be bought back by this man, who had, in fact, tried to sell us inferior goods.

During this period, another extraordinary power presented itself.

I don't know how else to describe this peculiar power other than to say that I started to see "movies." I would look at someone and suddenly see snippets from his life, as though I were looking at a home movie. Or I would pick up an object that someone owned and see scenes from the life of the owner. Sometimes I touched something old and would have a vision of that object's history.

For instance, in 1985 I went to Europe to help Jacques Cousteau assemble the marine electronics for one of his projects. While I was there, I flew to London to see a friend. As we were walking through the city, I stopped in front of the Parliament building to adjust my shoe and put my hand on a handrail. Suddenly, I smelled horses. I looked to my left and there was no one there, yet I could hear children playing. I looked at a place right in front of Parliament and saw people in clothing from the 1800s playing croquet. I look to my right and saw a horse standing next to me relieving itself. I began to say something to my friend, but he was no longer there. Instead, people dressed in nineteenth-century clothing and wearing derby hats were walking past me on the sidewalk.

I was frightened and didn't know what to do. Here it was, winter in London, yet people were playing croquet and wearing spring clothing from another century. I couldn't let go of the railing no matter how hard I tried.

My friend saw that I was in some kind of trance and tried to talk to me. When I continued to stare at my surroundings and didn't reply, he pulled my hand loose from the rail. I snapped out of it as suddenly as it had begun.

"I was seeing this area they way it used to be," I said. "I could see London in the nineteenth century."

This was not the first time something like this had happened. Right after being struck by lightning, as I lay in my hospital bed and people took my hand, I found that I was suddenly them in a certain situation. For example, I would see this person fighting with someone in his family. I didn't necessarily know what the fight was about, but I could feel the pain or anger that the person felt.

Once, a close family friend came to see me and rested her hand on my forearm. Suddenly the "movie" started. I could see her sitting at a dining room table arguing with her brother and sister over a piece of land that had been left to them in someone's will. She was offering them a small amount of money for their part of the land, knowing full well that it was worth much more. She was trying to cheat them. I later told members of her family what I had seen, and it proved to be correct.

Another time a friend came to visit who had kidney stones. I didn't know about this problem before he came into the hospital, but when he put his hand on my shoulder to say goodbye, I suddenly saw him curled up and squirming in agony on his living room couch as he waited for his stones to pass.

I told him what I had seen and it shocked him. "That's exactly what happened," he said. "I finally passed them just the other night."

From the very beginning I noticed that stressful situations and crises dominated these psychic flashes. If people were fighting with children or spouses, that is what I saw in these "home movies." Car wrecks, angry girlfriends, bad family situations, office conflicts, illnesses, and other forms of stress were always the focal point of my visions. It is still that way.

One time, for instance, I was selling a car to a man. He was a pleasant fellow in his late fifties who had the thick, strong fingers of someone who had done manual labor for many years. We talked about the car for a while before he decided to buy it, and he never hinted that there was anything wrong in his personal life. As soon as he agreed to buy the car and we shook hands on the deal, I could see that something was indeed wrong.

I suddenly found myself in his living room on the previous day in the midst of an all-out family dispute between his adult children and him. I could feel his anger at his children as they badgered him unmercifully about an apartment building he owned. They wanted him to sell it and give each of them a lump sum of money. He, on the other hand, wanted to make improvements on the property so that he could continue renting the apartments and use the money for his retirement.

There was a lot of greed underlying the conversation and very little concern for the father. The father knew that his children were thinking only of their pocketbooks, and the conversation quickly escalated into a savage family combat that left him feeling angry and hurt.

I could see all of this. As I stood in my front yard with this very pleasant man, I felt great sympathy for him. I decided to let him know how I felt.

"I hope this doesn't scare you too much," I said to him. "But I can read minds."

I then told him what his previous day had been like, complete with the painful emotions that had accompanied the argument.

"I feel for you," I said. "These people haven't done a thing to help you take care of this property, and now they want to steal it from you. They should be ashamed."

He left my house with more than a new car. At first he was shocked, but after we talked about the incidents of the day before, he felt greatly relieved. "Talking about personal matters isn't something I usually do," he said. "But I didn't have a choice this time."

When I first discovered these paranormal abilities, I used them in ways that I now consider to be dishonest. I was a tough one to beat at cards, since I knew what the other players were holding in their hands. I could predict the next song to come on the radio or jukebox about eighty percent of the time. And at one time I correctly predicted the winning team in football games 156 times in a row, including, in about eighty percent of those games, the scores.

I soon felt guilty about using these powers in such a way. I felt that they had a certain God-given aspect to them that made them holy. I abruptly stopped gambling and began looking for positive ways to use my psychic powers. Instead of betting, which was not spiritually fulfilling, I talked to others who were betting about pursuing more spiritually fulfilling activities than gambling.

Using one's psychic abilities to touch people spiritually often requires a gentle approach. (If all you want to do is perform parlor tricks, a frontal assault is just fine, since your aim is to shock the person.)

For example, I was in a restaurant one time when I noticed that my waitress had the burned-out look of someone who had not slept well for several nights. Her forehead was deeply furrowed, and she seemed angry and agitated.

Halfway through the meal she came by to refill my coffee cup. She rested her hand on the table while she did this, which gave me the opportunity to touch her hand. When I did that, the "home movie" started immediately.

I could see this woman talking to an older man. They were standing on a street somewhere, and she was trying to hold his hand. It was obvious that he wasn't very interested in her. As she talked to him, he kept turning away, looking down the street or at passing cars—anything to keep from looking at her.

For a moment I was her. I felt her pain at knowing that her relationship with this man was doomed. This scene and the knowledge came like a flash, and then it was gone.

When she returned to deliver the check, I stopped her. "You know, all older men aren't what they are cracked up to be," I said. "Sometimes you lose them no matter what you do. Don't blame yourself. You tried everything and now you feel like a fool. Actually, you were the best thing for him, and you know it."

The waitress was alarmed by my insight into her life. She looked at me like I was the devil. But when she realized I was harmless, she came back to the table.

"You're right," she said, sitting down. She revitalized before my very eyes in the few minutes we were able to talk.

When such events started happening with regularity, I told Raymond about them. We were sitting in a restaurant in Georgia when I told him that I could read minds. He clearly did not believe me. He asked me how I thought it worked, and I just shrugged.

"I don't know how I know the things I know, Raymond," I said.

I told him that I could see scenes from a person's life as though I were viewing a home movie. I gave him a few examples, but he was still skeptical.

"Okay," I said, feeling a little angry at being challenged. "You pick out somebody in this restaurant and I'll read her mind."

He picked our waitress, who was walking by the table at that moment. I asked her to stop and I took her hand. The "movie" started immediately. The first scene was of her arguing angrily with her boyfriend. They were sitting at a kitchen table and really going at it. I saw him grab his coat and leave. Then another snippet of film appeared. I could see the boyfriend holding hands with another woman, a blonde with long curly hair and a cute button nose. Then came a short piece of film that showed the woman with long curly hair standing at a bar with the waitress.

I told her what I saw. She was both scared and angry at the same time, scared of me and angry at her boyfriend. "That's exactly what I thought was going on," she said. "My boyfriend is seeing my best friend. Every time I confront him about it, he denies it and leaves. Finally I went out with her the other night and asked her about it, but she says it's not happening."

There was still doubt in Raymond's eyes, so I asked him to pick another person. Next to us was a woman in a booth who had been eavesdropping on our conversation with great interest. Raymond introduced himself and asked if she would mind holding my hand in the name of research.

When she did, another "home movie" popped into my head. In one scene, I saw this woman in a backyard with an elderly woman. They were happy and laughing, but the gaiety seemed forced, as though there were something frightening that they were trying to laugh away. The next scene was of these two women sitting together in a house. The woman whose hand I was holding was crying, and the older one looked worried. I could tell that the older woman was sick and that the younger one was worried that it might be a fatal illness.

I released the woman's hand and told her what I had seen. Her eyes moistened as she told me that her mother had cancer. Naturally she was worried, and there had been many nights like the one I described, in which she and her mother had spoken openly about the future.

I chose about five more people and told them a variety of things, including where they lived, what kind of car they drove, who their friends were, what their financial situations were, and what sorts of problems they were having.

These people reacted in different ways as I watched their "movies." A couple just gasped and covered their mouths. One angrily told me to stop. Another wanted to hear more, and one blushed and said that she felt as if she were suddenly naked.

Raymond finally believed that something truly extraordinary was happening. But we didn't understand the how and why of it, which was particularly hard on me, since I was the one who had to live with my abilities.

As I had told Raymond, I don't understand why I am able to see these "home movies" of people's lives, or why I hear sentences before they are spoken. Furthermore, I don't always like it. Having psychic abilities means that you have access to a person's most tender spots, the areas of his life that are most shielded from public view. "Seeing" these areas is sometimes good because it gives people a chance to talk freely about the pain in their lives.

The problem is that people don't always want to talk about the pain in their lives, least of all with a stranger who tells them things strangers shouldn't know. I have been accused of being a private investigator, a peeping tom, a thief, even someone who has access to private government files. I have been threatened and even slugged by people who didn't like me snooping around in their business.

Frankly, I can't blame them. Before I realized that things like this happened, I would have been upset if someone I didn't know accurately read my mind. Even though I know that what I do is going to upset some people, I still can't stop it from happening.

If there is any consolation in having psychic abilities, it is that other near-death experiencers have them, too. I don't mean just the experience itself, which is an intense psychic event. I mean what happens after the experience. I have yet to meet a person who has had a near-death experience who doesn't have flashes of precognition or very well-developed intuitive powers. It makes sense, since people who have had a near-death experience have had nature broken down for them into the very essence of life.

I have heard hundreds of near-death experiencers report psychic events in their lives. I once spoke to a Russian, for instance, who was struck by a car and sent to the morgue because he was believed dead. He was put into a refrigerated file drawer for three days, during which time his spirit left his body and roamed. He went home and saw his children and then went into the apartment next door where the couple's year-old child would not stop crying. They had taken him to the doctor several times, but no one could figure out what was wrong. This man's spirit was able to communicate with the child and discover that he had a hairline fracture in his pelvis.

The man was discovered to be alive just before the pathologist started his autopsy. He was sent to the hospital where he made a full physical recovery, but not, they thought, a psychological one. He kept talking about traveling out of his body and visiting family and friends. Finally, he asked that the neighbors be brought to him with their crying child. He said that he had talked to the child when he was "dead" and that the child was crying because his pelvis was broken. An X-ray showed that the man was correct.

"This whole thing was a psychic experience," said the Russian. "It has left me not understanding myself."

The most interesting example of psychic powers to come from a near-death experience was told to me by my co-author about a researcher named Frank Baranowski in Mesa, Arizona. In 1979 he had the opportunity to interview a bishop at the Vatican whose heart stopped for several minutes as the result of a heart attack. He had a near-death experience that was so startling to his fellow churchmen that Pope John Paul was summoned to his bedside.

The pope asked the bishop if he had seen God. The bishop wasn't certain. He had been greeted at the end of the tunnel by a stranger who had escorted him to a bright and loving light. The whole experience was just that simple, he told the pope, except that when he returned, he passed through the walls of the Vatican and went into the pope's dressing chamber.

"What was I wearing?" asked the pope.

The bishop perfectly described the garments the pope wore for his morning office.

After he returned to health, the psychic experiences continued. He was able to predict a number of things, including the heart attacks of two fellow church officials.

Were his psychic experiences and those of others like him caused merely by a heightened intuition? I don't know. I *am* sure that the notion of psychic powers seems farfetched to most people. It certainly does to me. It is hard for me to comprehend even my own case—how a bolt of lightning through the head and a journey to a spiritual world could make me psychic.

I have thought about it hundreds of times, and still it makes no sense. Is it possible that a near-death experience could cause a human being to develop extraordinary powers, even make it possible for him to read minds and see into the future? Before this happened to me, I would have laughed at the idea, as I would have laughed at the very notion of a near-death experience itself. But now it is the main question on my mind.

Luckily, others have pondered this same question in recent years and have come up with some remarkable answers. In

1992 Dr. Melvin Morse published the results of a major study on near-death experiences in a book entitled *Transformed by the Light*.

In this study, Dr. Morse conducted detailed examinations of hundreds of people who had survived near-death experiences. Using standard psychological tests, he discovered that they do indeed have more verifiable psychic experiences than the average population—more than four times the number, according to his study.

Most of these psychic experiences are simple and insignificant. For instance, many people have premonitions of telephone calls—they tell a co-worker or member of their family that a specific person is about to call, and in a few moments that person does. These calls usually come from close family members, but often they are from people they haven't heard from in years. Since they told other people before the event happened, they were verifiable psychic experiences.

Most of the experiences cited in his book go way beyond telephone calls, however. One woman dreamt that her brother was bleeding from his side and hands and was yelling for help. She told her family the dream in the morning and was told to forget it, that it was nothing but a nightmare. Yet within days, her brother was wounded in the side and hands by burglars in just the way she imagined it.

Dr. Morse cites dozens of stories like this in his study. Rather than ignore them or chalk them off to coincidence, he chooses to examine them more closely and concludes that there is indeed something about the near-death experience that makes people more psychic.

What this "something" is is a question I can't answer. Nobody can, as of yet. Some think there is an area of the brain that becomes sensitized by near death and that it is the area responsible for psychic communications. Others believe, as did Freud, that we communicated in a psychic fashion before we developed speech and that the near-death experience revives these psychic abilities.

I don't know why I have psychic abilities and I don't know why others have them either. I do know that things happen all the time that are intriguing yet unexplainable. To a large extent we live in a world that is still a mystery. To deny that mystery might be to deny the world at its best.

12
Rebuilding

By 1978 I was making a strong comeback. I could walk almost normally, and I could concentrate long enough to start thinking about rebuilding my life.

Being struck by lightning had cost me everything. I had lost my house, my cars, and my businesses, all to pay doctors and hospitals. All told, I had spent tens of thousands of dollars to stay alive.

By most people's standards, I was in bad shape. But by my standards, the ones I had adopted after the accident, I was a regular Olympian. My weight was still low, and I kept having disturbing blackout spells. My doctors said that these were caused by my damaged heart. They estimated that about thirty percent of it had been damaged, maybe even made useless, by the lightning. My heart had a "pumping insufficiency" that sometimes prevented enough blood from getting to my head. When that happened, I just collapsed.

Fortunately, there were people who were always there to pick me up. Sandy was still with me, as were friends like David Thompson, Jan Dudley, and Jim and Kathy Varn. When I collapsed in public, they were usually there to help.

The doctors were concerned that my heart would degenerate over time and eventually become a real problem. I didn't feel as though I had to wait for it to become a real problem, since it seemed like one already.

I had options, of course. I could sit around and wait, hoping that my heart would heal and I would make a full recovery, or I could go back to work. I decided to work. Because of my regular visions about the centers, I became fascinated with electronics. I started three businesses, all dealing with electronics.

The first was a business that sold a surge-suppressor—a device designed to prevent power surges from ruining household equipment. As you can imagine, I was the perfect salesman for this product, being a living example of what can happen to *human* equipment that receives too much electricity!

I also went back to work for the government, manufacturing and installing electronic anti-bugging devices in government buildings around the world. Called "masking systems," their function is to prevent eavesdropping.

The third business involved the manufacture of a piece of equipment that was shown to me in one of my visions—an electronic anti-fouling device designed to keep barnacles off the hulls of ships, thereby cutting down on added fuel consumption caused by drag.

This invention, which I developed with two friends, was a boost to environmental protection. Until then, the best way to keep barnacles off a hull was with a highly toxic paint. Now the same thing could be done by transmitting electrical tones through the hull. This invention thus doubled the benefit to the environment by increasing fuel efficiency and reducing toxic discharge into the waters.

I also did work with the deaf. I modified a piece of equipment called an audio transducer to convert speech into vibration. This device can be attached to any surface, including the human body. When music or sound is passed through the transducer, it vibrates and turns whatever it is attached to into a speaker. I would fit these devices to the back of a deaf person's ear, enabling him to "hear" through vibration. Helen Keller used a similar method when she put her hands on people's throats to feel them talk.

I remember one deaf woman who looked frightened as I hooked the device onto her ear. Her mother kept telling her it was all right, but she was afraid of what hearing might be like. I turned the transducer on and spoke to her. She looked at me and began to cry. "I can hear that," she said. "I have never heard anything before."

Deaf people suddenly being able to hear reminded me a lot of my sudden acquisition of psychic powers. For years they have learned to adjust to living in a silent world. Their other senses have compensated so well that they may not have realized they were missing anything. Then one day—wham!—like a bolt of lightning they are introduced to a world they didn't know existed. They are thrilled yet frightened, all at the same time. It is like exploring something they never knew existed.

The transducers were also shown to me in one of the visions that I was still having on a regular basis. I called them "hockey pucks" because that is what they reminded me of—little round black blocks. I didn't know what these hockey pucks were, but through the visions I knew that they were supposed to transmit music through the body of the person who was lying on the bed.

Through the visions I began to realize certain things about the human body, one of which being that, like these transducers, we transmit spiritual, mental, and physical essences of ourselves to the world around us. By learning to be in touch with our electrical and biological selves, we can make ourselves higher beings who transmit the spiritual side of life.

My visions about the centers were all about understanding the body—how it produces energy and how that energy can be found in such a way that it has a spiritual context to it. When you reach the point where you can control this energy and transform it into a positive force, you have found the part of you that is God.

The goal of the centers was to redirect human energy, but I didn't know that at the time. Rather, I was simply told to do certain things. I started the companies mentioned above because I was directed to do so by the spirits. I also started a company called Scientific Technologies, which manufactured electronic components.

I took on some partners in this last business. I explained to them that I wanted to start the business because I was being directed to do so by my visions. They believed me because they had known me for a number of years. They knew that before being struck by lightning, I didn't know much about electricity, but afterward, I was taught everything I needed to know about it by spirit teachers.

"I don't know why I am supposed to start this business, other than that I am being told to in my visions," I told my partners.

They agreed to follow the vision with me. I was told to direct the business toward the environment, and I did that by continuing to manufacture and install the anti-fouling systems on ships. For a while we didn't do well, and then the government banned the anti-fouling paint. They finally compiled enough scientific studies to realize that it was harmful to the environment. In fact, it was so dangerous that falling into Norfolk Harbor when the paint was in use required an immediate trip to the hospital to be detoxified. When the paint was outlawed, our sales climbed tremendously.

In 1983, I followed the vision away from marine electronics and went back to the de-bugging business. I have been in that business ever since.

And, of course, the visions continued. They were about kindness and finding the right components to create the centers.

I volunteered my time to hospice work, whose goal is to make people comfortable while they die, usually at home. I did this because I was directed to do so by the visions. I would visit patients and tell them my story. Many of them had never heard of the near-death experience. Being so close to death themselves, however, they were very interested to hear the account of a spiritual traveler, someone who had been where they were going.

Most people shun deathbed situations because they have an incredible fear of death and want to avoid it for as long as possible. I think if people spent more time around the dying, their fears of physical death would be allayed. I am not saying that death isn't frightening and hard to deal with, because it almost always is, but along with the pain and fear of letting go of the physical life comes an awakening of the spiritual.

As a hospice volunteer, I was involved in caregiving for the caregiver. Basically, this meant that I provided relief to the family member who was on deathbed watch. I like doing this kind of relief work because primary caregivers really need a break. They die a little bit each day and are usually overlooked by the other members of the family. Not only do they feel trapped, they often have a conflict with the person who is dying.

For example, I once helped a mother who was caring for a son dying of cancer. The first thing I did on approaching the deathbed was feel the patients pulse. I did this both to check the pulse itself and to see his "home movie."

This boy's "movie" was a bad one. I could see his mother standing by the bed with her hands on her hips and anger on her face. He was a captive audience to her harangue, and he was angry about it. I could feel surges of anger as she talked.

"Wow," I said to the boy. "What are you so upset about?"

"You won't believe it," he said. He then proceeded to tell me about his mother's guilt over his death. She somehow felt responsible for the fact that he was dying. Several times a day she stood over his bed and blamed his illness on things she had done. None of it made any sense, he told me. In the last couple of days it had become worse, because she had started blaming *him* for his illness, saying that he had done things to cause it.

"I'm dying of cancer," he said. "It's not her fault or mine. I'm just dying."

When the mother returned, we had a good discussion about guilt and death. I then told them my story, which seemed to put them at ease.

"Don't let death tear you apart," I told the mother. "You'll never forgive yourself."

On another occasion I went to a ranch-style house in a middle-class section of South Carolina. I was greeted at the door by a woman who was genuinely glad to see me. She was caring for her mother, who, she said, was a "little tough to get along with."

The daughter introduced me to her mother and abruptly left. I did what I always did—I took the woman's wrist and felt her pulse. Right away, the "home movie" started. I could see the two women embroiled in an argument that had taken place about ten minutes before I arrived. I couldn't hear what was being said, but I could feel it, and the feeling I got was that the woman who was dying was a genuine bitch.

"I don't know what it was that the two of you were fighting about," I said. "But this is really no time for it. This is a time to be kind instead of being an aggravating old woman."

I held her wrist again and could see that the source of this woman's anger was her husband. He had moved out one day and forced the sale of their house, leaving her with nowhere to live except her daughter's house. She hated living with her daughter, and her daughter hated having her there.

"Don't be mad at your daughter because of what your husband did," I said. "It isn't her fault."

The woman thought that her daughter had told me about the fight. I let her believe this, and we had a two-hour discussion about caring and love. Later, when the daughter came home, I told them how I really knew about their fight, and what it was like to be dead.

Nowhere has the use of my psychic abilities been more gratifying than in these deathbed situations. The dying can't afford the luxury of time, which allows a certain bluntness around the deathbed. If there is something to be dealt with, the dying prefer that it be dealt with right away. They want to get problems out in the open and solve them.

For example, I once went to a home where two parents were caring for their daughter, who was dying of breast cancer. The daughter was married and had two children, a fact that I could deduce from the pictures on the walls.

I went into the room where the daughter was and took her pulse. A scene flashed into my mind. I could see her at a doctor's office as the doctor showed her an X-ray. He was pointing to a specific area and talking very directly to her as she held her hand over her mouth. Then I saw her leave the doctor's office with no intention of returning.

In another scene I could see her husband reacting in anger as his wife told him that she had cancer. She looked sick in this second scene, which made me think it was some time after the visit to the doctor. I could sense a great deal of tension as they talked. Although she seemed to need tenderness, he volunteered none, only anger.

I knew what had happened, and I went straight for it.

"Can I ask you something Jane?" I said. "Why did you not go back to the doctor?"

"I just couldn't believe it so I ignored it," she said.

She began to weep softly as she told me that she couldn't face the thought of an operation. When the cancer worsened and her husband took her back to the doctor, he discovered that she already knew about the disease. By then it was too late. Her husband was so angry that he wanted nothing more to do with her.

"He's mad at me for not doing something about it," she said. "Now he is going to be left alone with the kids and everything, and he blames me for it."

"It's too late to worry about it," I said.

When the parents returned, I told them why their son-in-law was angry. They knew nothing about the earlier diagnosis. All they knew was that the husband was so angry he wouldn't even come and see his wife. At least now they understood what was wrong.

Unfortunately, this story doesn't have a happy ending. I went to the husband and tried to help him overcome his anger. He wasn't interested. He resented his wife to her dying day, and as far as I know, he didn't even attend her funeral. But at least I tried.

As I said, I was led to do hospice work by the visions. I was told to spend time around the dying so that I would understand it from the perspective of others. By doing this work I learned that stress reduction was the key to improving a person's death as well as life.

S ometimes I would marvel at the way things had gone since I was struck by lightning. Here it was, thirteen years later, and I was just beginning to feel as though I had climbed out of the grave. Physically I looked okay, although I really wasn't fine at all. I couldn't walk very far or fast without having to stop to catch my breath. I avoided stairs, mainly because climbing a couple of flights was as taxing to me as running a mile is to most people. I would stand at the top of the stairs and sweat profusely, panting to catch my breath.

My mental state had improved greatly. When the accident first happened, I would sit and jabber all day. If I wasn't talking about my near-death experience, I was talking about the mission the spirit beings had given me, the one that called on me to build the centers. I couldn't get them out of my mind, so that was all that came out of my mouth. I still talked about the experience a lot, but I no longer went on and on the way I used to.

Still, the visions were always with me. I was driven to complete the centers as quickly as I could. I knew how to make the visions real, except for the bed, which was still a mystery to me. The transducers that had appeared to me in the vision were revealed as resembling two hockey pucks put side by side. Other components of the bed appeared in these visions as well, and I was gradually recognizing what they were and finding them. The trick was to make sure that I had all the components and that they went together in the right way. I had been given a deadline of 1992 to complete both the bed and the centers, a deadline I felt I would meet without trouble since I was being guided by the visions.

Nevertheless, the accident and all the "baggage" that accompanied it weighed heavily on my personal life. Sandy and I finally divorced when the constant talk about the experience and the need to build the centers became too much for her. I couldn't blame her. Near-death experiences are hard on couples. With the constant visions and the psychic developments, added to the physical damage I had suffered, we had a surefire recipe for a failed relationship.

Despite all this my life was in relatively good shape. As I said earlier, I was just beginning to feel right again. But before I could even stand up and dust myself off, I fell right back down.

13

Heart Failure

I t was May of 1989, and I had been working too hard for a couple of years. When I wasn't in Charleston or nearby Aiken working my businesses, I was in Washington, D.C., installing anti-bugging devices in the Pentagon. Managing this part of my business alone kept me busy at least sixty hours a week.

In addition, I had the workload placed on me by the visions to contend with. To learn about kindness, I was told to continue my work as a hospice volunteer. I did that with no regret. I found great pleasure in helping people at the time of their greatest need. Even family members sometimes reject the dying, not because they don't love them but because they can't accept the sad facts of death.

For example, I noticed that one man had trouble approaching the bed of his mother, who was quite aged and dying of cancer. He and his family would come to visit her twice a day, but after a while the man would stand out in the hall while the rest of the family talked to his mother.

Finally I approached the man. He was reluctant to talk at first, almost hostile. Then I broke the ice by saying, "You seem to be mad at your mother." He looked at me as if I had revealed his deepest thoughts, but that wasn't the case at all. I think anyone who looked at this man could have seen the anger in his face. He was mad at death and angry at his mother for accepting it by checking into a hospice. He didn't like the idea that death would rob him of his mother, who was one of his closest companions. In a strange, almost inexplicable, way, he felt as though she were rejecting him.

"I don't want her to give up because I'll never see her again," he told me, emotion welling in his voice.

I told him that what he was doing was natural. I had seen it before. He had fallen back into the role of a child. Although he was an adult with a family and a good job, he was still his mother's little boy. And now that little boy was coming out and saying that if he didn't get what he wanted, he wasn't going to talk to his mother anymore.

"The problem here is this," I told him. "Your mother knows it's time to die, and she is facing it with courage. You need to stand with her because there is nothing you can do to change it. It is her time."

Then I told him about near-death experiences and my own

story. He was enthralled to hear death being presented as the beginning of a great adventure and not the end.

It was a healing moment for this man, who went back into the room and became a good son for the remainder of his mother's life.

It was a learning experience for me, too, and learning is why the spirit beings wanted me to work as a hospice volunteer.

I spent an average of twenty hours a week working in hospices and nursing homes, but sometimes quite a bit more. When patients were in their final hours, I would stay at their bedsides around the clock if they wanted me. That meant losing a lot of sleep, which wasn't really as important as the lessons to be learned from the dying.

Other parts of the visions drove me into overtime as well. I had been building versions of the bed since 1979, but I was still studying the components. I had found all of them by now but didn't quite understand how to put them all together. I continued to work hard on completing this puzzle, and the only way I knew to do that was to stay true to the visions.

Talk of these visions was becoming a burden to my friends. All too often I heard them say that I was crazy. For a long time they said it behind my back. Then they finally got to the point where they didn't care if I heard it or not. After one particularly rough week during which I could hardly keep my eyes open, a close friend said, "You want to get some sleep? Forget these visions and get on with your life. They are just in your way."

I couldn't have agreed more. The visions *were* in my way. I wanted them to go away more than anyone, but it wasn't that easy. I just couldn't ignore them.

All of this combined to make me work harder than I should

have. I began to falter. At first I found myself constantly exhausted. I would wake up tired and stay that way until I went to bed at night. Thinking it was a nagging case of the flu, I tried to sleep it off.

I rebounded briefly, but as soon as I resumed my arduous schedule, I began to slide again. I was driving hundreds of miles each week between my home and the Washington, D.C., area. I felt bad physically, but I had to keep working hard for the survival of my business. Still, I knew something was seriously wrong because my lungs felt clogged and I coughed all the time, but nothing came up.

The severity of the situation finally hit me when I found myself riding to Charleston with my partner Robert Cooper. I was pouring sweat. I lay down on the backseat, hoping that a little rest would make me feel better. It didn't. For the remainder of the day, I couldn't sit up without severe feelings of dizziness. "I must have pneumonia," I said to Robert.

I went to bed for a couple of days and actually felt better. However, as soon as I got up and tried to resume normal activities, my lungs got that hard feeling and I got worse.

I was sure I had a strain of pneumonia or the flu that I couldn't fight off. "They'll get rid of it in the emergency room," I said to another of my partners. She knew that going to the hospital was a big step for me because, as I always joked, "I don't like to go to hospitals because every time I go to one, I die." She helped me walk to East Cooper Hospital, which was only a few blocks away. By the time I arrived, I felt as though I had run a marathon. At the admissions desk I completed a form detailing my medical history, which took all of my remaining energy. Finally, the person at the admissions desk sent me straight to an examination room while my partner filled out the admissions forms.

"I think I just have the flu," I said to the examining physician, who looked with horror at my medical-history form.

I was fighting for breath by then, and it seemed as though my lungs weighed a ton. He listened to my heart and lungs with his stethoscope. His eyebrows went up a little as he did this. Then he called for a nurse and had her bring in an electrocardiogram machine. He and the nurse quickly hooked the electrodes up to my chest and ran off a tape that looked like one of those graphs of the stock market. He examined the tape for a moment and then sent it off to be examined more carefully by a specialist.

He didn't leave my side. He helped me on with my shirt, watching me all the time in a way that made me nervous. When the specialist's report came back, he left the curtained-off area where I was sitting to read it. When he returned he seemed even more nervous than when he had left.

"Do you want me to tell you the truth?" he asked.

"Nothing but the truth," I said.

"Well, you do have an infection that is causing pneumonia," he said. "But I am afraid that you are almost in cardiac arrest. If we don't get you into this bed and off to intensive care, you'll be dead in about forty-five minutes."

I appreciated his bluntness and thought that it showed real courage on his part. Most doctors beat around the bush before telling a patient he is doomed. But this one didn't mess around, probably because of the severity of my condition. I suspect by the way he hovered close to me that he thought I would die of fright, but what did I have to be frightened of? I had died once already and liked it. I was ready to go back. It was a relief to know that in less than an hour I would be dead.

As the doctor hovered close to me, I decided to bring some levity into the room. I smiled at him. "Well damn doc," I said. "Don't you think I ought to lie down?"

For the next several hours I became the center of attention. An IV was started, and I was given massive amounts of antibiotics. Doctor after doctor came and listened to my heart. I was treated to a variety of tests, including a painful one known as cardiac catheterization, in which they ran a tube up to my heart through an artery in my leg and squirted dye directly into its chambers so they could view it on a television screen.

They only did that test to see precisely what shape my heart was in. They already knew what the problem was: I had picked up a staph infection through a cut on my hand. At first, the infection made me feel like I had the flu. When I ignored it, I got pneumonia. Then it headed straight for my weakest spot, my lightning-damaged heart. There it settled into my aortic valve, chewing it up until it couldn't seal anymore.

The lightning had already reduced my heart's pumping ability by almost fifty percent. Now, with the valve damaged and leaking, I was drowning in my own blood. As a result, I was in great pain. I was gasping for breath, coughing up blood as I struggled for air. The antibiotics were making me sick, and the constant prodding and poking of the medical staff seemed more like a nuisance than a help. Still, I was in a good mood, keeping a smile on my face through all of the grim proceedings. I knew I was going to die, and I wasn't unhappy with that.

"You know, doc, death is okay. It's just getting there that hurts."

"Excuse me?" said one of the doctors, looking up from his clipboard.

"I've died before and it was really quite pleasant," I said. "It's the getting there that hurts."

"I can see that you have died before," he said, looking at my medical records. "People don't often survive something like being struck by lightning, not when their heart stops for as long as yours did."

"I'm sorry I did survive, doc. It was great over there. I didn't want to come back."

"Don't worry," said the doctor. "We'll try our best to keep you alive."

"You don't understand," I said to the doctor. "I want to die. I've been there and it's beautiful. Since I came back it seems as though I've been in confinement. In heaven you're free to roam the universe."

The doctor looked at me for a moment and saw the smile on my face. I think it unnerved him because he immediately waved to a nurse at the station outside the room.

"Nurse," he said. "Take Mr. Brinkley's temperature, please. I think he has a fever."

I made it through the night.

My good friend Franklyn had called my father, and he

started a telephone chain. By morning, my family was gathered in the hospital. Soon the room was filled with people who could barely contain their emotions at the sight of me.

Illness has its interesting moments, and one of them is the way you are regarded by other people. I had experienced stares of disbelief when I was struck by lightning, but this time I was conscious of my surroundings and able to enjoy much more the effect my appearance had on others. It was almost as though I were a movie screen and the people who came into the room were watching the gruesome parts of *The Exorcist*.

I can't blame them, because what they saw was pretty frightening. I was charcoal-blue right down to my fingernails. The sheet around my head was stained with the blood I coughed up. Every breath was a struggle because my lungs were filling with fluid, and they rattled when I exhaled.

It was eerie for people to be around a deathbed whose occupant was so cheerful. Still, I couldn't help it. I told my dad that it was just a matter of perspective. "For you it's like I am leaving and I'll never be back," I told him. "For me it's like I am going home."

A nurse came in with forms for me to sign. I looked at them and realized they were consent forms that would allow surgery to be performed on my heart. A couple of surgeons had told me that the only way I could survive would be if they tried to replace my aortic valve with an artificial one. I told them that I was ready to die and didn't want to have surgery, but they ignored me. They had the forms prepared anyway, assuming that I would change my mind.

"I ain't gonna sign them," I said. "I'm gonna let God decide this one."

Two surgeons came into the room. They had stern, matter-of-fact looks on their faces as they stood by the bed. One of them laid out the facts while the other stood and watched.

"The longer you wait, the less chance you have of surviving surgery," he said.

"Good, because there isn't going to be any surgery," I said.

"If we don't operate on you within about ten hours, your heart will be too weak for us to do surgery," he persisted.

"Great," I said. "Then I'll get to die."

I saw my father in the corner of the room talking to Franklyn. Soon she pulled away and left the room.

"We'll leave the forms here," said the surgeon. "You can sign them if you change your mind."

In a few minutes, Franklyn came back. She spoke to my dad for a few seconds, and then they both came over to the bed.

"Franklyn just called Raymond," my father said. "He's on his way."

I was glad to hear that he was coming. He had been in Europe for several weeks on a speaking tour. He didn't know until that call that I was in the hospital or even that I was sick. According to Franklyn, he was catching a flight from Georgia and would arrive in a couple of hours. I would have a chance to see him one more time before I died.

And so we waited. I don't remember much of what was said, but I do remember what I was thinking: *Now I won't get a chance to finish the centers. I was supposed to have one completed by 1992, but it doesn't look as though I'm going to make it that far. Today I am going to die.*

After a couple of hours had passed, Raymond came into the room. What he saw clearly shocked him. There were four people standing around the bed with grim and frightened expressions as I made jokes and tried to lift their spirits. Raymond stood with them and tried to act nonchalant.

"You aren't looking so great," he said in his gentle manner. "The doctors here can fix you up."

"I don't want to get fixed up," I said. "I just want to die."

Being the good doctor, Raymond persisted. "Is there anything I can do to make your last hours more pleasant then?" he asked.

"There is one thing you can do," I said to Raymond. "You can go down to Arby's and get me a roast beef sandwich with lots of horseradish. I want to go out on a cholesterol rush."

We all laughed, I so hard that blood began running out of my nose. Then Raymond and I began talking about how we met and about all the people we had talked to. He said that all near-death experiencers claim they no longer have a fear of death, but that this was the first time he had actually seen that lack of fear demonstrated.

"How come you're not afraid?" he asked.

The answer came easily: "Because living on earth is like being forced to go to summer camp. You hate everyone and you miss your momma. Raymond, I'm going home."

Raymond tried to console my family and friends. I could hear them talking, but I wasn't paying much attention at this point. I was organizing things in my mind, trying to determine if there were any loose ends that I had to tie up before leaving this world.

Finally, Raymond came back to the bedside.

"You don't have to die," he said. "Stay for me. I need your help."

Raymond had a wonderful and understanding smile on his face and a pleading tone in his voice. It made me feel wanted and needed, a basic human desire to which I found myself susceptible. "Okay," I said. "Give me the forms."

As soon as I signed them, the surgical team took over. Someone cut a hole in my neck and inserted a tube. Someone else cut a hole in my leg and inserted a tube that they pushed all the way to my heart.

By then I was so weak that the doctors at East Cooper decided to transport me to Roper Hospital, where they perform more high-risk surgeries. They kept me there overnight, hoping I would improve, but when I didn't, they decided to go ahead with the surgery.

I don't remember much after arriving at Roper. I remember a nurse coming in to shave me. Then I remember looking down beside the bed and seeing green surgical booties walking next to me as I was wheeled to surgery. Then there was a man in a green mask who gave me two shots in the rear. "That'll relax you," he said.

Then there was blackness.

14

The Second Time
I Died

I saw blackness but heard voices.

"I don't have a good feeling about this one."

"I hear you. He has an infection, he's weak, his heart was damaged by lightning, he isn't in very good physical shape. It's a challenge."

"I'll bet you ten bucks he doesn't make it."

"You're on."

I rolled over out of the blackness to face the stark brightness of the operating room. I saw the two surgeons and the surgical assistants who were betting on my survival. They were looking at my chest X-rays in a lighted box and waiting for the prep work to be done on me so they could see who would collect on the bet. I looked down on myself from a place that seemed to be well above the ceiling. I watched as they held my arm out straight and strapped it to a stainless-steel brace.

A nurse painted me with a brown antiseptic and then draped me with a clean sheet. Someone else gave me a shot directly into the IV tube. Then a man with a scalpel made a clean, straight cut the length of my breastbone. He peeled back the skin. An assistant handed him a device that looked like a small saw, and he hooked it under my breastbone. Then he turned it on and sawed my chest open. A spreader was inserted into the cut and my ribcage was pried open. The envelope of skin that surrounded my heart was cut away by another doctor. At that point I was treated to a firsthand view of my own beating heart.

I don't remember seeing any more. I rolled back away from the surgery and into a position that left me engulfed in blackness. I could hear chimes ringing, three sets of three with a tone at the end of each of them. In the darkness a tunnel opened. The walls of this tunnel were grooved like furrows in a freshly plowed field. These furrows ran the length of the tunnel toward the bright light at the end. They were silver-gray, speckled with gold.

After seeing the opening of my own chest and hearing the doctors place bets on my survival, I knew there was no way I was going to live. Yet instead of being frightened, I was relieved. My body had been a burden to me since it had been struck by lightning. Now it was gone. I was free to roam the universe once again.

At the end of the tunnel I was met by the Being of Light,

the same one that greeted me the first time. People often ask if these Beings have faces. Neither time did I see a face, just a brilliantly glowing spirit that was firmly in charge of me and knew where I was supposed to go.

He drew me toward him, and as he did he spread out, almost like an angel spreading its wings. I was engulfed by these wings of light, and as I was, I began to see my life all over again.

The first twenty-five years passed as they had in my first near-death experience. I saw many of the same things: the years of being a bad child, my growing up and becoming a bad-assed soldier. Watching these early years again was painful, I won't deny that, but the agony was tempered by viewing the years since the first experience. I had a feeling of pride about these years. The first twenty-five years were bad, but the next fourteen were of a changed man.

I saw the good that I had accomplished with my life. One after the other, events both great and small were reviewed as I stood in this cocoon of light.

I watched myself volunteering in nursing homes, performing even the smallest duties, like helping someone stand up or comb her hair. Several times I watched as I did jobs no one else wanted to do, like clipping toenails and changing diapers.

One time for instance, I helped care for an elderly woman. She had lain in bed so long that she was stiff and could hardly move. I scooped her out of the bed like a child—she couldn't have weighed more than eighty pounds—and held her while the nurses changed the sheets. To give her a change of scenery, I walked around the building with her in my arms.

I knew this meant a lot to her at the time because she

thanked me profusely and cried when I left. Now, as I relived the event, the perspective I had in this heavenly place let me feel her gratitude at having someone hold her again.

I relived a time in New York when I invited a group of bag ladies to a Chinese restaurant for dinner. I saw these women in an alley scrounging through garbage cans and felt compassion for their situation. Escorting them into a small restaurant, I treated them to a hot meal.

When I saw this event again, I could feel their mistrust of me as a stranger. Who was this man and what did he want? They were unaccustomed to someone trying to do a good deed. Still, when the food came, they were grateful to be treated with humanity. We stayed in the restaurant for almost four hours and drank several large bottles of Chinese beer. The meal cost me more than a hundred dollars, but the price was nothing compared to the joy of reliving it.

I saw painting and collage contests that I had helped organize for mental patients at a hospital where I volunteered my time. Because my girlfriend worked as a psychiatric social worker at the same hospital, I had a chance to participate in an experiment that came back to me in this life review.

It was a simple one, really. We wanted to take several mental patients to church. Most of these patients were from the Deep South and had been raised singing church hymns. Why not bring them to church, we reasoned, to see if the hymns could tap a sane place in their minds?

We took about twenty patients to a large Presbyterian church and had them sit in the back row. By the end of the service, many of the patients were singing hymns that they had sung in the years before mental illness took control of their lives. Some of these were people who hadn't even spoken in ten years.

While reliving this experience, I felt how going to church had helped ground these mental patients in the real world. I felt the good feelings they had experienced as they drank punch, ate cookies, and relived the good old days they had had in church before something went wrong in their minds and they got so weird.

I saw people I had cared for who were suffering from AIDS. In scene after scene, I watched as I helped them carry out daily tasks such as getting a haircut or going to the post office. In this review I felt the importance they placed upon not being condemned by others for the crime of loving somebody. At one point my review dwelled on a specific incident—the time I helped a young man deliver the very difficult news to his family that he had AIDS.

I saw the two of us as we walked into his parents' living room. He had asked that his entire family gather for this announcement, so the room was filled with his parents, his brothers and sisters, and even a couple of aunts.

We took a seat in front of them, and he blurted it out immediately: "Mom, Dad, everybody, I have AIDS."

There was shock all around the room as his words sunk in. The mother immediately gasped and began to cry, and the father walked out the front door and stood in the front yard to be alone with his grief.

Everyone in the family had known for some time that something was wrong with this man because he looked sick and had recently lost a lot of weight. But no one dreamed he had AIDS.

This was an extremely painful confrontation that didn't turn out well. The man was rejected by his father, who could not accept his son's homosexuality. The mother, too, had little to do with her son after this announcement. As I relived the event, I could feel the family's shame and humiliation at what they had just heard. At the time I was angry with them because they didn't react the way I thought they should. But now I could sympathize with them because I could feel how they felt and knew that it was a sincere shock to hear this frightening news. Nothing in their lives had prepared them for something like this.

After we left the living room, he was devastated. We had talked about this moment of confession many times. He wanted to come clean with his family and had sincere hopes that they would accept him. The rejection he felt in that room was like a spear through his heart.

I felt terrible about the family's reaction. I, too, thought they would accept their son. Had I made a mistake in encouraging him to tell his family? Should I have told him to keep it secret? Frankly, I felt sick at the time.

"Listen," I told him as he wept during the car ride back to the hospital. "You're gonna die. You had to do it to keep yourself honest and pure. You finally got it out and that is honorable."

I had doubts about everything I did in connection with this case. I even went back to the man's parents and begged them to be forgiving in their son's final days. Still I felt guilt, as though I had helped facilitate a disaster.

But now, as I relived the event and could feel everyone's emotions, I knew I had done right. Even though there was agony on the part of everyone involved, in the end he felt that he had revealed that hidden part of himself to his family and could prepare to die in peace:

The life review that came with this second near-death experience was wonderful. Unlike my first, which was filled with mayhem, anger, and even death, this one was a pyrotechnic display of good deeds. When people ask me what it is like to relive a good life in the embrace of the Beings of Light, I tell them it is like a great Fourth of July fireworks display, in which your life burst before you in scenes that are spiced with the emotions and feelings of everyone in them.

After the life review was over, the Being of Light gave me the opportunity to forgive everyone who had ever crossed me. That meant that I was able to shake the hatred that I had built up against many people. I didn't want to forgive many of these people because I felt that the things they had done to me were unforgivable. They had hurt me in business and in my personal life and made me feel nothing for them but anger and disdain.

But the Being of Light told me I had to forgive them. If I didn't, he let me know, I would be stuck at the spiritual level that I now occupied.

What else could I do? Next to spiritual advancement, these earthly trespasses seemed trivial. Forgiveness flooded my heart, along with a strong sense of humility. It was only then that we began to move upward.

The Being of Light was vibrating. As we moved upward, that vibration increased, and the sound emanating from the Being became louder and higher-pitched. We moved up through dense fields of energy that changed color from dark blue to a whitish blue, at which point we stopped. Then the Being's pitch lowered and we moved forward. Again, as in the first experience, we flew toward a range of majestic mountains, where we dipped down and landed on a plateau.

On this plateau was a massive building that looked like a greenhouse. It was constructed of large panes of glass that were filled with liquid in all the colors of the rainbow.

As we passed through the glass, we also passed through all of the colors contained in the liquid. These colors had substance to them and felt like fog off the ocean. They offered a slight resistance as we entered the room.

Inside were four rows of flowers, long-stemmed beauties with cup-shaped petals the consistency of silk. They were every color imaginable, and on each of them were drops of amber-colored dew.

Among these flowers were spirit beings wearing silver robes. These were not Beings of Light. I can best describe them as radiant earthlings. They moved up and down the rows of flowers, emitting some kind of power that caused the flowers to become brighter in color as they passed. These colors would leave the petals and beam through the panes of glass, sending back a rainbow of colors. The effect was like being in a room surrounded by ten thousand prisms.

I found this environment to be tremendously relaxing. The colors and surroundings combined with the humming vibration of the Being to erase stress. I remember thinking: *Here I am, either dead or dying, and feeling good about it.*

The Being of Light moved close to me. "This is the feeling you are supposed to create in the centers," he said. "By creating energies and tones in the centers, you can make people feel the way you feel right now."

I became aware of the fragrance of the flowers. As I breathed in the scent, I heard a chant resonating throughout the building. A-L-L-A-H-O-M went the chant, A-L-L-A-H-O-M.

This chant made me aware of everything around me, and I began to breathe the fragrance deeply and observe everything with such intensity that it was almost as though I were bathing in it. A-L-L-A-H-O-M, A-L-L-A-H-O-M, went the chant, and I became more and more absorbed in my surroundings. As I did I began to vibrate at a speed equal to everything around me. I became one with everything around me and could experience everything. At the same time, everything was experiencing me.

As I delved into this heavenly world, it also delved into me. There was an equality to the experience. Not only was I *given* a heavenly experience, I was *giving* one. As I was blending with this place I call the heavenly realm, it was also blending with me with the same amount of respect, courage, hopes, and dreams. I was an equal to all things there. I realized that true love and understanding make us all equals. Heaven is that kind of place.

I would gladly have stayed there. I had smelled the heavenly fragrance and had seen myself among the essence of all things. What more could I ask for?

I looked at the Being of Light, who knew without a doubt what I was thinking. "No, you're not staying this time," he told me telepathically. "You have to go back again."

I didn't argue. I looked around and took in a view that time will never erase from my mind. The room was crisscrossed with colors that radiated from the liquid-filled panes. In the distance I could see jagged mountains that were every bit as beautiful as the Swiss Alps. The chant that resonated through the room was as beautiful as a symphony. I closed my eyes and bathed my ears in the sound. The fragrance was wonderfully overpowering. I took a deep breath . . . and I was back in my body.

I passed through no transition zone this time, and the change was very abrupt. It was like being in Buckingham Palace, blinking, and suddenly finding yourself in a garage.

I looked around the room and saw other people covered with powder-blue sheets. The room was very bright, and everyone in it had tubes in his body that were attached to bags or machines. I could tell there were tubes down my throat and needles stuck in my arms, and I felt as if there were lead in my head and an elephant sitting on my chest. On top of all this, I was freezing cold. Good God, I thought, I feel worse than before the surgery.

"Where am I?" I asked a nurse.

"You're in the recovery room," she said.

I closed my eyes and didn't remember anything for another eighteen hours.

Something happened in the recovery room that I don't remember at all. Franklyn told me this story and the doctor confirmed it.

Shortly after surgery was completed, one of the surgeons noticed that I was oozing blood from around one of the tubes. He kept an eye on it for some time and then called another doctor in. They decided that they would have to go back in and try to stanch the bleeding surgically.

Franklyn was standing there listening. When she heard that they were considering another surgery, she pushed by them and kneeled down next to my head. "Dannion, the doctor says you are bleeding and they are going to have to cut you open again and stop it. You can stop the bleeding, Dannion, I know you can. Try to stop the bleeding."

The doctors stood there for a while and watched. Within a few minutes, the bleeding stopped. And then, said Franklyn, they just looked at each other and walked out of the room.

W ithin a few days I had recovered enough to sneak out of bed and take a shower. A few days after that, I was able to put on street clothes and sneak down to the hospital cafeteria for a good meal.

As I sat there eating fried chicken, the surgical assistant who had bet that I would die came in and sat at a table next to me. I introduced myself and then told him what I had seen and heard as they prepared to cut into my heart.

He was unnerved by what I told him and even went so far as to apologize for making such a bet when I was still "awake."

"That's quite all right," I said to him. "In a way I wish you had won the bet."

15

To Be Continued

My heart surgery did not make me physically whole again. I was released from the hospital in a few weeks, but in many ways it was like going from the frying pan into the fire. Sometimes I still pass out when I exert myself even slightly. I have often turned blue and been forced to lie down in the middle of restaurants or department stores because my heart wasn't pumping as it should. For a long time I could count on blacking out at least twice a week. I finally learned how to recognize the danger signs and sit down before falling. That saved me several bloody noses, but I still black out about once a month.

Some of my medications make me extremely susceptible to infections, and the high dosage of blood thinner I am on makes an ordinary cut bleed like a mountain stream.

In the summer of 1993, I cut my finger and contracted a staph infection that kept me bedridden for almost a month. Despite being given massive doses of antibiotics intravenously, I almost went into septic shock. For days I wanted to die, not so much to visit the heavenly place again, but because I was in such physical pain that I could hardly stand it.

Through all of these physical trials, the visions have sustained me. Although I no longer "attend" the celestial classes where the Beings of Light taught me about building the centers, I have remembered my lessons well and plan to have the first one built very shortly.

In 1991 I completed the bed, which is the most important component of these stress-reduction centers. I erected it at Dr. Raymond Moody's clinic in rural Alabama. He was just beginning to study facilitated apparitions, a method by which bereaved people can have visionary encounters with departed loved ones. To achieve the state necessary for these encounters, the patient has to be extremely relaxed. After trying the bed himself, Raymond decided that it was an excellent way for his patients to relax quickly.

We used the bed with many people, and the results often went far beyond relaxation. Patient after patient reported experiencing intriguing forms of altered states. Some saw kaleidoscopic visions of color, others felt so relaxed that, as one person put it, "I felt like I imploded." The most common altered state reported was an out-of-body experience.

Now that I have been able to test the bed in a clinical setting,

I can concentrate on establishing the centers. I am working on the first of these in South Carolina. The focus of this first center will be to help the terminally ill face death. Seventy cents of every dollar spent in health care in this country is spent in the last six months of a patient's life to extend life an average of fourteen days. Those are the most horrendous days of a dying person's life and are certainly among the most difficult for his or her family.

I think it's important for people to avoid a painful death. I am not advocating suicide, just common sense. Unnecessary life support builds false hopes and prevents people from making a smooth and spiritual transition. It is also devastating for their families, who can pour all of their financial and spiritual resources into keeping a loved one alive just a few days longer.

Having died twice, I know that the world that awaits us when we leave here has a lot to offer a terminally ill person. That is why this first center will be a hospice, one that helps the dying person make the transition while helping his family cope with the pending loss. The center will be a place of laughter and deep relaxation, a place where people can heal their spirits and build a strong faith in God.

Many people have asked me why I am so relentless about these centers.

"Listen," I say. "Thirteen Beings of Light told me to build these centers. They put it on me. They didn't ask if I wanted to build them, they just told me that that is what I had to do. When I pass, I will be with them forever. Knowing that, I am determined to pull it off."

In the last few years, I have spoken to millions of people around the world about my two near-death experiences. At the invitation of Boris Yeltsin, I appeared on Russian television with Dr. Moody and spoke to millions of people in that country alone about my experiences and visions. I was even able to talk about my belief in spiritual capitalism—that all people should be free to worship the way they choose. There are many paths to righteousness, I said, and that is good news for all of us, since no one seems to be on the same path, as far as I can tell.

I know that the path I am on is a unique one. I am frequently told this by the people I meet. Once, after speaking to a church group about my life, a woman approached me with a look of puzzlement on her face. She had heard many people speak about God, she said, but never one quite like me.

"I'll bet you drink," she said.

"Yes ma'am, I do."

"And you obviously like women, don't you?"

"Yes ma'am, I do."

"Then I will say this, Mr. Brinkley," she said, giving me the evil eye. "When God was looking for prophets, he must have been scraping the bottom of the barrel to have found you."

I couldn't agree more. I only have to look into a mirror and see the man I have become to be totally baffled by all that has happened.

Why me? I often ask. Why did this kind of thing happen to me? I never asked for it to happen. I never got on my knees and asked the good Lord to change my life. Why me?

To that question I have no answer. Still, in my search for consolation, I frequently find myself reading I Corinthians, especially chapter 14, which contains some of the most powerful writing in the Holy Bible. In that chapter can be found two verses that give me comfort:

> For he that speaketh in an unknown tongue speaketh not unto men, but unto God; for no man understandeth him; howbeit in the spirit he speaketh mysteries.
> But he that prophesieth speaketh unto men to edification, and exhortation and comfort.

I don't know why I was chosen to do what I do. I only know that my work is to be continued.

About the Authors

DANNION BRINKLEY lives in South Carolina, where he does hospice work and assists Dr. Raymond Moody at his research center, the Theater of the Mind. PAUL PERRY is the coauthor of the widely acclaimed bestsellers *Closer to the Light* and *Transformed by the Light* (Piatkus) and has written more than ten books on a variety of subjects. In 1988 he received a fellowship from the prestigious Freedom Forum Foundation at Columbia University. Perry was also the executive editor of *American Health* magazine, and his writing has appeared in a number of publications, including *Rolling Stone*, *Men's Journal*, and *Reader's Digest*. He lives in Scottsdale, Arizona.